T0300031

The Profit of Peace

Corporate Responsibility in Conflict Regions

Karolien Bais and Mijnd Huijser are the founders of Logos Research, a consultancy working with multinational enterprises in conflict regions that are willing to match their corporate goals with local needs for stability, prosperity and peace.

Karolien Bais is an investigative reporter, specialising in international relations, development co-operation and military peace missions. Born in Indonesia, she has lived in the Antilles, Nigeria and the Netherlands and has been a travelling journalist working for Dutch media and press agencies since 1972. She has published articles, surveys and books on conflict-ridden countries including Nigeria, Mozambique, Nicaragua, Cambodia, Bosnia-Herzegovina, Israel/Palestinian Territories, Sri Lanka and Afghanistan.
www.businessdiplomacy.biz

Mijnd Huijser is senior consultant in cross-cultural management and managing director of CMC–Culture & Management Consulting. Having lived and worked for 15 years in Southeast Asia, the Middle East and France, he has gained considerable experience in international business and inter-cultural co-operation. He specialises in cross-cultural communication, confidence building and conflict management. In the Netherlands he has worked with 'culture gurus' Geert Hofstede and Fons Trompenaars as a cultural awareness trainer for *Fortune* 500 companies. Among his current clients are 3M, Accenture, Canon, Clifford Chance, Nissan-Renault, Philips, Unilever and the Clingendael Institute for International Relations.
www.cmc-net.org

THE PROFIT OF PEACE

CORPORATE RESPONSIBILITY IN CONFLICT REGIONS

KAROLIEN BAIS and MIJND HUIJSER

Routledge
Taylor & Francis Group

LONDON AND NEW YORK

First published 2005 by Greenleaf Publishing Limited

Published 2017 by Routledge
2 Park Square, Milton Park, Abingdon, Oxon OX14 4RN
711 Third Avenue, New York, NY 10017, USA

Routledge is an imprint of the Taylor & Francis Group, an informa business

Cover by LaliAbril.com.

British Library Cataloguing in Publication Data:
   A catalogue record for this book is available from the British Library.

ISBN 9781874719908 (pbk)

Contents

Acknowledgements 6

Foreword 7
  Patrick C. Cammaert, Military Adviser, Department of
  Peacekeeping Operations of the United Nations

Preface 10

Chapter 1
MULTINATIONAL CORPORATIONS AND CONFLICTS 12

Chapter 2
ETHICS AND CULTURE 26

Chapter 3
ENTERPRISE AND GOVERNMENT 38

Chapter 4
CLEAN HANDS AND FAILING STATES 54

Chapter 5
POWER AND PRIVILEGE 72

Chapter 6
CARROTS AND STICKS 87

Chapter 7
PROFITS AND IDEALS 101

Chapter 8
SCENARIOS AND STORYTELLING 117

Bibliography 127

Useful websites 132

Appendix: map of conflict regions 135

Index 138

Acknowledgements

Many people have taken time to share their experiences with us. We would like to express our special thanks to Ron Aston (Premier Oil), Patrick Cammaert (UN), Arno van Dijken (ING), Peter Frankental (Amnesty International Business Group), Jarno Hill (Australian Embassy, Rangoon), Jeremy Hobbs (Oxfam International), Jean-Louis Homé (former Director, Heineken), Olivier de Langavant (Total), Jean-Michel Lorne (French Embassy, Rangoon), Carlos Alberto Montaner (Cuban author and journalist), Ms Hông-Trang Perret-Nguyen (former ILO representative), Bernard Pe-Win (Business Forum), Leon de Riedmatten (Humanitarian Dialogue), Frank Smithuis (Médecins sans Frontières), Alexander Tarnoff (Save the Children US), Ms Ma Thanegi (Burmese author and journalist), U Thein Tun (MGS Beverages), Sein Thun (Hu Pin Hotel), Jan Bouke Wijbrandi (Novib) and Luc Zandvliet (Corporate Engagement Project).

Foreword

The current eagerness of multinational companies to invest in Iraq is hardly ever found in African countries emerging from war. Sometimes the economic and strategic interests in a country are so large that the international community is spurred to intervene—as in the Democratic Republic of Congo or in Sudan. But other countries are left drifting in the marsh. The few hundred million dollars set aside for Liberia, Sierra Leone or Ivory Coast contrast sharply with the $87 billion for the reconstruction of Iraq. Yet the African countries have good prospects for investments, especially if the security situation is stabilised.

Peace and stability are vital for a country to emerge from the marsh. People will only start cultivating their land if they are certain that they will not have to flee again before the harvest. Demobilised warriors need an income-producing job as soon as they come out of the bush, or they will soon reach for their weapons again to supply an income. Police, army and judiciary need to be reformed to prevent the country from slipping back into the social chaos from which it has just emerged.

The United Nations, together with other organisations, is often called in to help establish peace and stability, but it will need the co-operation of private enterprises. It is my strong conviction that the first priority is developing the economy through creating jobs and providing education and vocational training, which leads to prosperity. Of course, multinational corporations are not philanthropists; without profit they will vanish. But their impartial presence can fan economic recovery and, when implemented cautiously, can have a stabilising effect. Multinational corporations are indispensable to drain the marsh and give the country's inhabitants dry feet.

Of course, investing in conflict regions has its drawbacks. There are hardly any countries to be found where the political climate is completely clean or where someone with a Western view will not come up against any moral obstacles. During my UN assignments, I found it striking that some countries are quite open to investments whereas others create a no-go area for multinational corporations. As commander of the UN force in Ethiopia/Eritrea (2000–2002), I noticed the huge potential of the fishing grounds and its breathtaking oceanic world for economic development of the region. But the Eritrean government failed to provide incentives for investors.

Again, during my assignment in Cambodia (1992–1993), I saw great possibilities for investments. The country had suffered severely from the Khmer Rouge regime. In my sector there was only a single railway, which, not unlike the roads, was barely useable. My great wish was that some donor country, organisation or enterprise would open up the country by renovating the railway, roads and bridges, of course in close consultation with the local authorities. It could have done wonders in revitalising the local economy. Given the cheap labour, such an initiative would have instantly provided work for many people. Another project I dreamed of was getting tourism started. With relatively small investments a large part of the population could have made a living. In my encounters with the former warring parties, I often brought up this kind of subject. It was not easy to get in touch with groups like the Khmer Rouge, but they reluctantly accepted emergency projects for which the UN forces provided some money. These projects laid the foundation of mutual trust which resulted in the Khmer Rouge slowly abandoning their occupied territories and which gave a modest boost to the local economy.

Investing in conflict regions is trying. It requires perseverance and necessitates solving many ethical problems. But, if asked for advice, I would say: lay down your Western view, keep in touch with the local authorities, be practical, and don't shy away from sometimes unreliable regimes. Other companies, probably with lower standards, will not hesitate to fill the gap. Co-operation between the national government, tribal leaders, the UN, non-governmental organisations, embassies and multinational corporations is very important. Each sector can provide its specific capacity to solve the problems. This, in broad outline, is the strategy that is now being used to pull a failing state such as Liberia out of the marsh. It is a strategy I would welcome for many other conflict regions.

This book, containing many examples of good efforts, is an important contribution to developing such a strategy.

Major-General Patrick C. Cammaert
Military Adviser, Department of Peacekeeping
Operations of the United Nations

Preface

How can multinational corporations, operating ethically in conflict regions, contribute to stability and peace? This was the leading question in our search for the experiences of multinational corporations in troubled countries such as Rwanda, Afghanistan and Burma.

Two factors appeared to be significant. First, MNCs in conflict regions are confronted with dilemmas in which cultural differences play an important role. Neglecting this will at best lead to ineffectiveness and at worst bring new conflicts. Second, ethically justifiable decisions do not necessarily produce ethically justifiable results. Both aspects also cause great tensions between civil organisations and companies, whereas at the same time the need for these parties to work closely together is becoming more and more essential.

It was not our objective to judge which of the parties in conflict regions are right or wrong. Rather, we wanted to find out what attitude ultimately contributes most effectively to conflict prevention or stabilisation of a region. In other words, in this book we have measured corporate responsibility by the results and not by the intentions.

All the CEOs we interviewed were well aware of the fact that their companies operating in conflict regions would always influence the conflict one way or another. This awareness in itself is quite extraordinary, and it shows that the indifferent comment 'business is business' by and large belongs to a past era. Also extraordinary was that the managers allowed us a glimpse into their private world, since this candour makes them all the more vulnerable to criticism. Non-governmental organisations (NGOS) closely scrutinise MNCS, and often for good reasons. It is their role to jump into action whenever an MNC acts unethically. That is no doubt a valuable contribution to a better world. But we found that NGOS that regard the corporate world as by definition untrustworthy risk acting to the detriment of their own ideals. We were happy to speak with representatives from the not-for-profit sector who are well aware that there are new ways to realise their ideals, and acknowledge the untapped potential of MNCS.

Through the accounts of the interviewees and of other managers who have experience in conflict regions, we have been able to identify the ingredients for an approach that leads to a solution of conflicts and to more stability. Only in the long run will we be able to measure the success of the new profession of 'business diplomat', but in the meantime the day-to-day business practices of MNCS show that they can work on 'the profit of peace'.

Karolien Bais and Mijnd Huijser
Spring 2005

1
Multinational corporations and conflicts

It may seem a strange notion to give the private sector a role in conflict prevention or resolution, but multinational corporations (MNCs) do have some characteristics that make them suitable companions in a well-tailored strategy for peace and stability. Their presence in a country can give incentives for prosperity, for rebuilding society and its institutions, and for improving respect for human rights. Their role is not mediating between warring factions, with one eye on the Nobel Peace Prize, because that requires an expertise truly beyond the core business of an MNC. It is precisely through performing its core business that the private sector can foster stability in a country or region.

Economic development is not the only condition for peace and stability, but it is central to reducing the global incidence of conflict (Collier *et al.* 2003; see Fig. 1.1). Rebellion and full-blown civil war occur only if they are financially rewarding. If a country reaches a higher level of prosperity, people have so much to lose that they will think twice before joining a movement that by definition leads to destruction. Most civil wars are fought in the poorest countries, economically dependent on natural resources. Controlling the export of these resources is an extremely lucrative business and in itself an incentive for violent takeovers. With these 'conquered' sources of income, the war can be amply financed and prolonged. When a larger diversity of sources of income can be created, controlling one of them becomes less attractive.

Direct foreign investments can boost jobs, training and technological innovations. MNCs have a strong potential to open up a country or region and have a positive influence on political systems. According to research by the World Bank, this applies not only to democratically governed countries but also to weak or autocratic regimes (Gissinger *et al.* 2002).

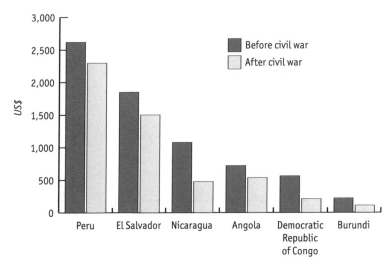

FIGURE 1.1 GDP per capita before and after civil war

Source: Collier 2003: 14

Through their operations, their human resources policies and their access to high-level political leaders, MNCs can set meaningful standards for people whose lives have thus far been dominated by weapons and arbitrariness. That is not an easy process. It implies the capacity to get to the bottom of local political relationships, cultures and traditions, and necessitates a well-directed strategy. But it is achievable.

To be clear, this has nothing to do with charity, like building a school for the community or facilitating scholarships for bright young students. Those actions do not really help to alleviate complex conflict situations. We would like to stress that MNCs can contribute to preventing or solving conflicts through their *core business* (see Figs. 1.2 and 1.3).

Past ignorance

This book is not a song of praise for MNCs in general. There is an abundance of hair-raising accounts of companies that feel no shame

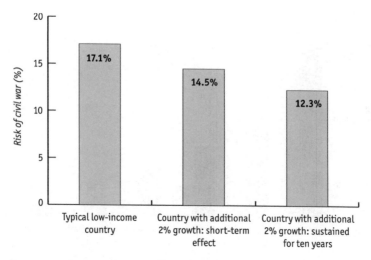

FIGURE 1.2 Improved economic performance and the risk of civil war

Source: Collier 2003: 67

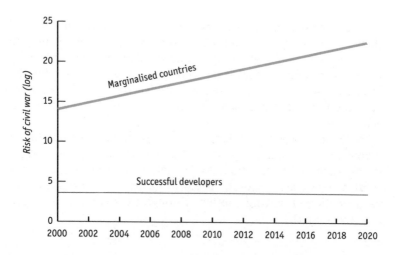

FIGURE 1.3 Development of risk of civil war for marginalised countries and successful developers, 2000–2020

Source: Collier 2003: 103

in profiting from conflicts by trading weapons or illegal resources, that prolong war by supporting one of the parties, that are in a war-torn country only because the lawlessness suits them well. Even companies that refrain from such criminal activities cannot be envisaged as potential peace builders if they profit unscrupulously from cheap labour or cheap subcontractors. Instead, this book is about corporations that are compelled to ethical, responsible entrepreneurship; companies that balance their desire for profit with compliance to international business and human rights standards and with a genuine investment in local workers, environmental protection, social development and stability.

Worldwide about 60,000 MNCs work in over 70 conflict regions. They operate in regions where social unrest is harshly repressed, where outright fighting takes place or where violent combat has recently ended. Whatever the attitude of MNCs and whatever their area of business, they influence conflicts or are themselves influenced by conflicts. Even if they do not directly invest in or trade with a conflict region, they always risk being associated with those conflicts (see Fig. 1.4).

Take ABN Amro,[1] one of the world's leading diamond banks. ABN Amro does not invest in Sierra Leone—it does not even have an office or a cash dispenser there—but it does grant loans to diamond traders. Some of these traders might well buy their raw materials from rebels, thus giving them the means to buy a new load of Kalashnikovs. In 2000 ABN Amro was targeted by international non-governmental organisations (NGOs) for its role in the trade in 'conflict diamonds'.[2] The matter demonstrates that a powerful, expert opponent has emerged that will not cease to point out their corporate responsibility to multinational enterprises. Heineken, Shell, Talisman, Nike, Reebok, Unilever and a wide range of other MNCs have met with this opponent. Supported by rapid means of communication, pressure groups are able to mobilise public opinion to accuse companies. They can put pressure on governments to prevent MNCs from doing business with reprehensible regimes. Also shareholders and employees bang the drum; they force the company leadership to account for their investments and operations.

1 ABN Amro ranks fourteenth on the world list of banks.
2 Research revealed that there was no evidence that ABN Amro financed traders in conflict diamonds but the bank did not sufficiently try to inspect the exact origin of the diamonds.

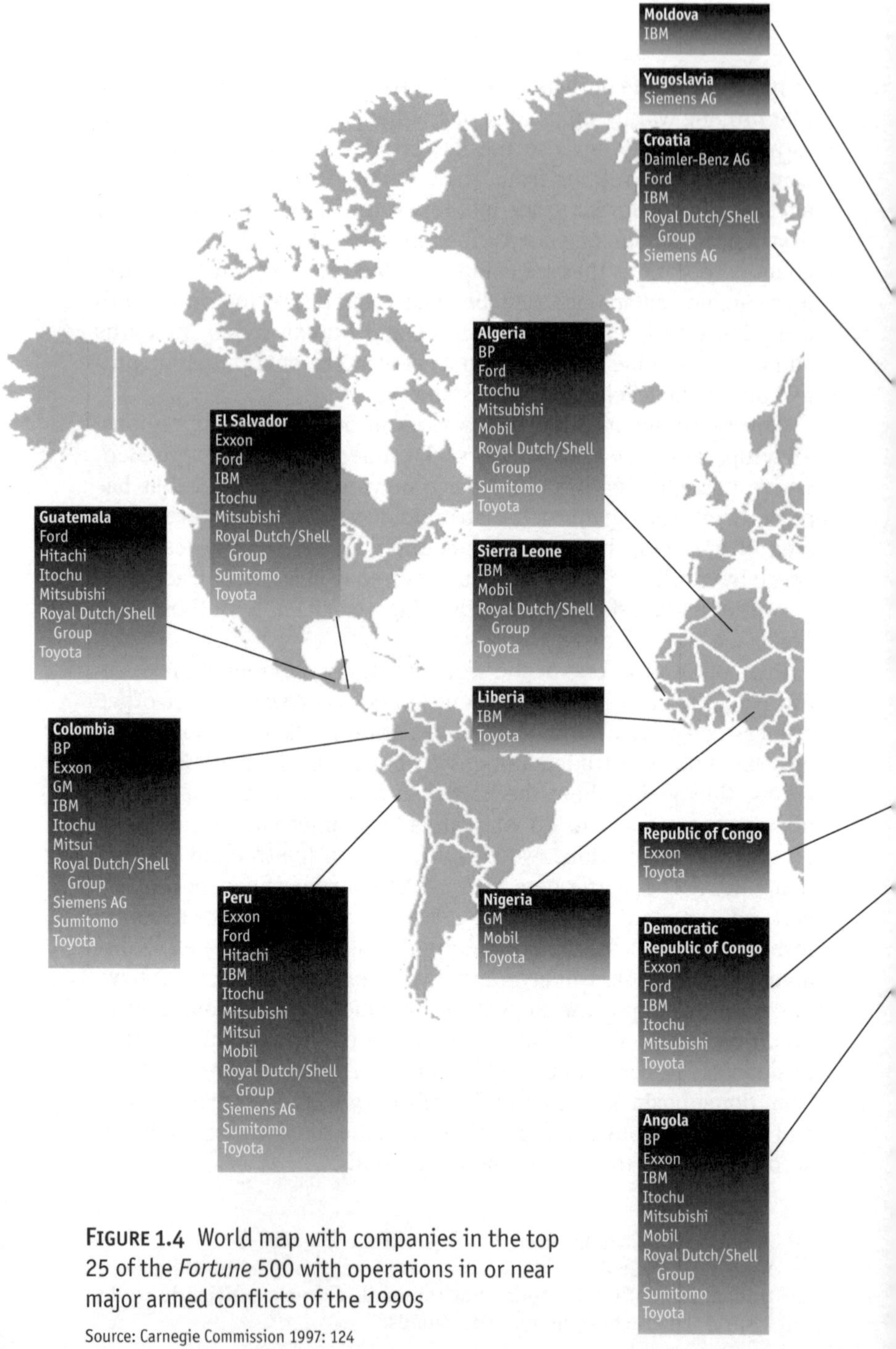

Moldova
IBM

Yugoslavia
Siemens AG

Croatia
Daimler-Benz AG
Ford
IBM
Royal Dutch/Shell
  Group
Siemens AG

Algeria
BP
Ford
Itochu
Mitsubishi
Mobil
Royal Dutch/Shell
  Group
Sumitomo
Toyota

El Salvador
Exxon
Ford
IBM
Itochu
Mitsubishi
Royal Dutch/Shell
  Group
Sumitomo
Toyota

Guatemala
Ford
Hitachi
Itochu
Mitsubishi
Royal Dutch/Shell
  Group
Toyota

Sierra Leone
IBM
Mobil
Royal Dutch/Shell
  Group
Toyota

Liberia
IBM
Toyota

Colombia
BP
Exxon
GM
IBM
Itochu
Mitsui
Royal Dutch/Shell
  Group
Siemens AG
Sumitomo
Toyota

Republic of Congo
Exxon
Toyota

Peru
Exxon
Ford
Hitachi
IBM
Itochu
Mitsubishi
Mitsui
Mobil
Royal Dutch/Shell
  Group
Siemens AG
Sumitomo
Toyota

Nigeria
GM
Mobil
Toyota

**Democratic
Republic of Congo**
Exxon
Ford
IBM
Itochu
Mitsubishi
Toyota

Angola
BP
Exxon
IBM
Itochu
Mitsubishi
Mobil
Royal Dutch/Shell
  Group
Sumitomo
Toyota

FIGURE 1.4 World map with companies in the top 25 of the *Fortune* 500 with operations in or near major armed conflicts of the 1990s

Source: Carnegie Commission 1997: 124

Turkey
BP
Ford
GM
IBM
Itochu
Mitsubishi
Mitsui
Mobil
Royal Dutch/Shell
  Group
Siemens AG
Sumitomo
Toyota

Azerbaijan
BP
Exxon
Ford
Mobil
Sumitomo

Russia
AT&T
BP
Daimler-Benz AG
Exxon
Ford
GM
Hitachi
IBM
Itochu
Mitsubishi
Mobil
Royal Dutch/Shell
  Group
Siemens AG
Sumitomo

Pakistan
Ford
IBM
Itochu
Mitsubishi
Royal Dutch/Shell
  Group
Siemens AG
Sumitomo
Toyota

Iraq
Sumitomo

Tajikistan
IBM

India
BP
Daimler-Benz AG
Exxon
GM
Hitachi
IBM
Itochu
Mitsubishi
Royal Dutch/Shell
  Group
Siemens AG
Sumitomo
Toyota

Sri Lanka
Ford
IBM
Itochu
Mitsubishi
Royal Dutch/Shell
  Group
Sumitomo

Philippines
BP
Ford
Itochu
Mitsubishi
Royal Dutch/Shell
  Group
Siemens AG
Sumitomo
Toyota

Cambodia
Itochu

Sudan
Ford
IBM
Royal Dutch/Shell
  Group
Toyota

Gulf Region
BP
Chrysler
Daimler-Benz AG
Ford
Itochu
Mitsubishi
Mobil
Siemens AG
Toyota

Indonesia
BP
GM
Hitachi
Itochu
Mitsubishi
Mobil
Nippon Telegraph
  and Telephone
Siemens AG
Toyota
Wal-Mart

Uganda
Ford
IBM
Royal Dutch/Shell
  Group
Toyota

Lebanon
Ford
IBM
Itochu
Sumitomo

Rwanda
BP
IBM
Toyota

South Africa
BP
Chrysler
Daimler-Benz AG
GM
Hitachi
IBM
Itochu
Mitsubishi
Royal Dutch/Shell
  Group
Siemens AG
Sumitomo
Toyota

Burundi
Toyota

Yemen
Exxon
Ford
Itochu
Mitsubishi
Royal Dutch/Shell
  Group
Sumitomo
Toyota

Chad
Exxon
Royal Dutch/Shell
  Group

The example of ABN Amro also illustrates that MNCs are opening themselves up to criticism. ABN Amro allowed its operations to be researched, and sought advice in adjusting its methods. And the bank decided to terminate relations with any client dealing in 'conflict diamonds'.

MNCs can no longer claim ignorance about local political circumstances. If they are still not aware of them, it is because they choose to be ignorant. Neither can they hide from the media, and hence from public scrutiny. The tiniest island in the Pacific, the most remote mine in Congo, the most obscure logging area in Brazil, every spot on earth can be covered by cameras. Moreover, companies are starting to realise that they should apply the same standards of responsible entrepreneurship abroad as they do at home. Indians suffering from illegal drainage of waste by Western companies know that these companies would risk high fines in their home countries, and the Indian victims find their way to court. Jurisdiction also globalises, as is demonstrated by Burmese fugitives living in Thailand, who brought a case to court in the US against an American oil company. They demanded compensation for allegedly having been forced to work on a pipeline in their homeland, Burma.

Self-interest

It is not only a moral stand that motivates MNCs operating in conflict regions to devote themselves to peace and stability. They have a stronger incentive: self-interest. This is all the better because self-interest outlives any trend or fashion.

Companies operating in conflict regions are faced with tremendously high expenses due to loss of vehicles and products, 'taxes' and protection money for local armed forces, security measures for their plants, loss of productivity caused by blockades, temporary evacuation of personnel, deterioration of the commercial climate, or even complete divesting. MNCs are constrained to diminish the risks and costs of doing business in conflict regions.

Companies that invest in a country for decades have a special interest in continuity and are compelled to minimise interruptions of their operations. What they need is what is currently called a 'licence to operate', a broad social acceptance of their presence. As Peter

Hain, leader of the British House of Commons and at the time Minister of State at the Foreign and Commonwealth Office, stated in May 2000 at a Business and Peace Conference:

> New opportunities have arisen from the reduced economic commercial participation of the state in most countries. And from globalisation. For business, this has meant huge transfers of resources to private sector management. With this expanded role come greater responsibilities. And higher expectations for business to do more for the well-being of a broader group of interested parties.[3]

Increasing corporate responsibility can even lead to greater profits, as was demonstrated in a study from the British Institute of Business Ethics (Webley and More 2003). Companies with a public commitment to ethical conduct perform better financially in the long term than those that do not. High ideals have proven to be in the self-interest of MNCs.

A substantial trend

United Nations Secretary-General Kofi Annan has discerned the importance of the private sector for development, stabilisation and peace. With his Global Compact, launched in 2000, he spurs companies to devote themselves to development in co-operation with governments, UN organisations, trade unions and NGOs. This Global Compact has grown into a network with hundreds of participants from all the sectors Kofi Annan envisaged. Even the international umbrella organisation of trade unions, ICFTU, which has never had much sympathy for employers, joined the initiative. And when the Global Compact network chose as one of its first topics the role of the private sector in conflict regions, Bill Jordan, Secretary-General of ICFTU stated:

3 Business and Peace Conference, organised by International Alert, Prince of Wales Business Leaders Forum (PWBLF), and the Council on Economic Priorities (CEP), London, 3 May 2000.

> We share the interest of the UN in exploring private con-
> tributions to improving prospects for peace in conflict
> zones. Trade unions are among the rare social institutions
> that can pull together people around their common
> interest as workers who would otherwise be in conflict.
> All three Compact partners should work together to help
> create an environment where productive investment and
> engagement can contribute to both stability and democ-
> racy.[4]

Four years after the start of the Global Compact, an independent assessment (UN Global Compact 2004) showed it has had a consid-erable influence on corporate policies in relation to the human rights, labour and environment principles. One of the conclusions of the assessment was that the Global Compact has helped spread the acceptance of business collaboration throughout the UN network and helped promote innovative intra-UN partnerships.

In April 2004, the then German CEO of Siemens AG, Heinrich von Pierer, was invited to address the UN Security Council on the subject of business and peace. Von Pierer, a dedicated advocate of a com-bined effort by business and international agencies to bring peace in conflict-prone regions, also spoke on the involvement of Siemens in the reconstruction of Iraq and Afghanistan. In his speech to the UN he said

> Alone, business could not change the world. But together
> with public partners, business could make decisive con-
> tributions in the struggle against violence, against anar-
> chy and against terrorism—and for civilization, freedom
> and for prosperity.[5]

The popularity of an organisation such as the World Business Coun-cil for Sustainable Development (WBCSD) is another sign that the imperative to direct their core business toward economic develop-ment, without social or ecological abuse, is starting to dawn on companies. About 170 MNCs from all industrial sectors have become members, which commits them to provide business leadership as a catalyst for change toward sustainable development and to promote

---

4   Bill Jordan on the CorpWatch website, www.corpwatch.org, 29 January
    2001.
5   UN Security Council, 4,943rd Meeting, 15 April 2004, www.un.org/
    news/press/docs/2004.

the role of ecological efficiency, innovation and corporate social responsibility.

One of the organisations that specialise in conflict resolution, the British-based International Alert, states that 'conflict sensitive business, and its promotion by public policy-making institutions, could become an important part of a collective effort to reduce conflict' (International Alert 2003).

International Alert is positive about the fact that large Western corporations have started to pay more attention to human rights, the environment and other areas of corporate social responsibility, but it warns that their understanding of conflict and corporate-conflict dynamics 'remains under-formulated, and constrained by a lack of skills and experience' (International Alert 2003).

There is a substantial trend for MNCs to try the path of conflict prevention or resolution either on their own or in co-operation with others. It may involve individual projects, such as that undertaken by the Norwegian oil company Statoil to facilitate the education of the judiciary in Venezuela in protecting human rights, or the initiative of seven Belgian MNCs that installed a fund in 2002 to enable aid organisations to start socioeconomic projects in post-conflict countries such as Mozambique and Nicaragua.[6]

There are also examples of a concerted effort to tackle the source of a conflict. An example is the explosive matter of coltan mining in Eastern Congo. There is much money to be made in coltan,[7] and all warring parties in the region know it. In 2001 a UN panel named and shamed the Rwandan army, the Ugandan military-commercial network, Congolese and Zimbabwean businessmen and a long list of Western companies for prolonging the war by looting resources, destroying the landscape and chasing the population off their land. One of the companies, accused of illegally obtaining elements, was the German H.C. Starck.[8] The company contested the allegation but nevertheless immediately ended all its import of the raw materials from Central Africa. The final report of the UN panel, released in

6 In Mozambique, Bekaert, Corona-Lotus, Interbrew, Koramic Building Products, Sidmar, Siemens and Union Minière financed projects of local organisations to lobby for international debt relief. In Nicaragua, demobilised soldiers, policemen and teachers are trained in conflict prevention.
7 Coltan is a mix of the minerals columbite and tantalite used, for example, in cell phones.
8 H.C. Starck has been owned by Bayer since 1986.

2003, exonerated H.C. Starck. In the meantime, in the summer of 2001 the British NGO Dian Fossey Gorilla Fund had contacted H.C. Starck with the explicit request to maintain its activities in the region. Their reasoning was that, as long as coltan is in the ground and people see a chance of earning money, the trade will not stop, so perhaps a regulated means of exploitation could be found that would benefit the population and the environment. H.C. Starck was willing to explore this possibility and sought like-minded international NGOs, UN institutions and MNCs. This led to the so-called Durban Process, in which the Dian Fossey Gorilla Fund co-operates with Congolese government officials, local officials in Eastern Congo, specialised NGOs, aid organisations, representatives of the population, the UN and MNCs. They have called in the expertise of a South African organisation that specialises in conflict resolution.[9]

Dilemmas

Whatever MNCs undertake in conflict regions, they will always be faced with dilemmas. Every now and again they will have to choose between two possibilities with both positive and negative aspects. Striving for ethical entrepreneurship, they will have to weigh these possibilities. For this book we interviewed CEOs who have had to deal with complicated decisions inherent in the following dilemmas:

- In conflict regions MNCs can be compelled to take over public tasks: infrastructure, healthcare, education, sometimes even tax collection. This undermines the already weak position of the government and some areas may benefit more than others, which can lead to new conflicts. By the same token, a responsible corporation cannot close its eyes to the social problems in its area of operations.

- One might say that it is ethically just to invest in failing states because raising prosperity contributes to stability. One might also be of the opinion that it is ethically just if companies get out of these countries. But in neither situation can a company keep its hands clean. When investing, a

---

9   For details see www.durbanprocess.net.

repressive regime benefits from joint ventures and tax levy. When divesting, a company will leave thousands of jobless people behind, while at the same time other companies will fill the gap, possibly companies that will be less scrupulous regarding labour and environmental standards.

• Ethical entrepreneurs are right to avoid countries in which they will be obliged to make use of undemocratic power structures. But it is also ethically justifiable to engage in business in these countries with the aim of contributing to the development of a war-torn region and to be pragmatic in relation to the present power structures.

• Economic sanctions are a frequently used means to bring about change in bad regimes. However, they are seldom successful and meanwhile cause much human suffering. If MNCs circumvent an economic boycott, they act unethically. But the consequences of complying with such a boycott also tend to be unethical.

• Many problems in conflict regions can be solved if companies co-operate with NGOs. But lack of trust between these two sectors is sometimes overwhelming and makes them unlikely partners. They also seem to have conflicting targets: the enterprise goes for profit, the NGO for ideals. Neither wants to compromise.

Cultural intelligence

To be effective 'peace builders', MNCs will have to make contact with the local population, local officials and (international) civil-society organisations. Of vital importance in these relations is 'cultural intelligence'. Without a keen sense of the differences in management styles, in perceptions of ethics and morality, and in the values behind political opinions, every peace effort is doomed to fail.

As many companies have experienced, ignoring the prevalent cultural values in conflict zones can not only lead to sordid situations but can fuel conflicts instead of quelling them. Instant solutions for problems, however well intended they may be, often have harmful side-effects. Oil drilling in the Niger delta in Nigeria has grown into a nightmare, partly because the local culture has over and over again been neglected. Shell has increased its contribution of money for social and economic development of the region to $60 million a year, but, instead of resulting in prosperity for the local population, this aid has brought about increased corruption and lawlessness.[10] The instant solution of paying compensation to the local population for the harm done to their fishing waters or farmland is in itself appropriate, but unwanted side-effects are that saboteurs deliberately destroy the environment in order to collect compensation. This has become a 'war industry' in itself: local warlords have created militia to steal oil, and the income is used to buy weapons. Clashes between gangs are often presented as an ethnic conflict, but in reality these gangs fight to enlarge their territory.

It is precisely the lack of 'cultural intelligence' that blocked a successful role for foreign companies to foster peace in Iraq. For foreign businesses to contribute to the reconstruction of the country the first and most important condition is to be trusted by local stakeholders. But the Iraqi Governing Council appointed by the occupying powers after the latest Gulf War, in the steps taken to revive the economy and boost the private sector, have not shown sensitivity for the need to build trust, nor for the local diversity of cultures (see also Amnesty International 2003c; Nelson and Moberg 2003). The biggest portion of the reconstruction money went straight into contracts with foreign companies, adding to their profits and not to the prosperity of local firms and the local population. When starting their operations in Iraq these foreign businesses expected to be welcomed and trusted, since they had come to bring 'Western' freedom and prosperity. But they were soon perceived by the Iraqis as profiteers, stealing *their* money out of the country. Rebuilding trust in order to gain the necessary legitimacy to operate is a huge task, considering the trauma of dictatorship, sanctions, wars and occupation (Newton and Culverwell 2003).

It is indispensable for ethical entrepreneurship to pay attention to culture. Ethical notions comprise values and norms that are culturally biased. This thought alone is enough to make people very restless, because ethics are considered to be universal and to exceed

10   The independent consultancy WAC Global Services warned in June 2004 in its report 'Peace and Security in the Niger-delta' that Shell might be forced to retreat completely from the area if ethnic conflicts escalate.

national cultural values. This is certainly true for some values. Everyone, regardless of cultural background, will condemn torture. Nevertheless, the European countries, Turkey, the US, Israel and China, to mention just a few, appear to have different ideas about what exactly torture is or when it is apparently acceptable to serve a transcendent goal. Without sliding down in a dangerous culture relativism,[11] companies in conflict regions will have to deal with the fact that they will inevitably meet with differing conceptions of ethics. If Western companies unwaveringly promote their own values, they can be accused of ethical colonialism.[12] Asian political leaders are very vocal in expressing their opposition to this Western attitude.[13]

Companies can become involved in situations that ask for exceptions to ethical rules. They will then have to consider if the end justifies the means. To be able to deal with this dilemma, companies will have to incorporate all cultural aspects into their considerations, as well as into the way they communicate their decisions to their stakeholders.

11 Culture relativism states that ethical values are a product of Western culture, hence not simply applicable in other cultures.
12 Culture evolutionists defend the notion that cultures evolve, that there is a hierarchy among cultures, and that Western culture is on the top. This notion has at one time been used to explain why Western colonial politics were ethically justified.
13 The Indian economist and Nobel Prize winner Amartya Sen states that many Asian leaders wrongly refer to Asian values to justify their autocratic performance. Human rights and tolerance, writes Sen, have their roots as much in Asian as in Western tradition. But Sen also criticises Americans and Europeans who tend to think that matters such as political freedom and democracy are rooted in Western culture and are hard to find in Asia.

2
Ethics and culture

In early 2003 the Canadian oil company Talisman Energy Inc. sold its share in an international consortium in Sudan. This decision was preceded by heavy pressure from the Canadian government, which had insisted since 1999 that Talisman should put its weight behind efforts to stop the civil war that had been dragging on in the country for decades. Pressure also came from international human rights organisations, which accused Talisman of providing income for the Arab–Islamic government, thus fuelling the war against the Christian and animistic rebels in the South. The UN Human Rights Commission in Geneva joined the chorus of criticism. Talisman saw itself confronted with a sharp decline in the value of its shares and retreated from Sudan, four years after arrival. The Indian Oil and Natural Gas Corporation took Talisman's place in the consortium.[1]

Talisman faced a difficult decision in Sudan. The company did not feel entitled to undertake peace initiatives ('we are not a sovereign government', Talisman stated in the press), but on the other hand didn't wish to be tainted by the scorched-earth tactics of Khartoum. One could say that it was ethically justified of Talisman to divest. However, one could also make out a good case for continuing operations. The retreat of Talisman would not hamper the use of oil as a source of revenue for the Sudanese government because the newly composed consortium would take up its old routine. The harm would fall completely on the local population. Talisman had brought relative prosperity to the 50,000 people in its employment zone by providing wells, schools, clinics and a modern hospital. The Asian

---

1 The consortium further consists of the Malaysian Petronas, the China National Petroleum Corporation and the Sudan National Petroleum Company.

partners in the consortium, however, do not feel compelled to provide basic social services. They are less strict in applying environmental or labour standards. They are less transparent in their external communication and therefore are not sensitive to pressure from activists. Hence, continuing its operations would also have been an ethically justified option for Talisman.

Entrepreneurs in conflict regions are regularly confronted with this kind of dilemma that demands an ethical solution. Multinational corporations (MNCs) willing to play a stabilising role in conflict regions will always be faced with considerations that are not easily compatible with norms and values based on Western ethics.

Ethics are about right conduct. The principles of ethics are not exclusively Western; they are to be found in all societies, including the non-Christian. But cultural differences play an important role in the interpretation of these principles.

In the debate over Talisman's presence in Sudan, values such as 'freedom' and 'justice' outweighed a value such as 'increasing the living standards of the local population'. The opinion of the local labour force, or even of the majority of the Sudanese people, was less important than these Western heavyweight values. Completely neglected was a value such as 'stability', which would have promoted the consideration of an option to give responsible MNCs a role in a well-designed strategy to obtain peace.

Politics

Cuba is a fine showcase of how foreign policy of different countries is culturally biased, although they share the same principles. The economy of the island is in distress. The main cause lies within the economic policies of the Communist government, but part of the harm has been done by over 40 years of American embargoes on trade and investments. The embargoes, meant to dethrone the 'despot', have not brought this aim any closer. Instead, the majority of the Cuban population spends most of its productive time on gathering the meal of the day, whereas the position of their president remains unchallenged. He can even arrest and execute dissidents at random, as he demonstrated again in the spring of 2003.

The European Union and the United States choose different political strategies. Both are founded in the ethics that the repression executed by the Castro regime is not to be tolerated. The EU refrains from measures such as boycott or isolation because it believes in influencing through a dialogue with the government and the civil society. The basic line of EU policy is that to be influential one should keep communicating. Bringing up matters such as the violations of human rights is only possible if a relationship has been established or at least some kind of understanding has been created. Not only do the Europeans prefer communicating instead of threatening, they also envisage stimulating economic activities as a means to open up Cuban society—to create work and knowledge exchange, hopefully leading to a stronger middle class that will be able to execute countervailing power against the dictatorship.

In the approach to the Castro regime, the cultural differences between the US and the EU are obvious. The US believes that the population is assisted by punishing the dictator who tramples on their basic rights. The Europeans, in general, prefer to enable the population by delivering humanitarian aid and creating better incomes, and at the same time by trying to 'seduce' or persuade the unjust regime into more respect for human rights. In Asian and African cultures one will hardly ever find leaders that presume to punish a foreign power, and if they do, the punishments will be limited in severity and length of time. Their preference lies in the opposite: rewarding good behaviour.

All of these preferences have nothing to do with the proven success of a certain method; they are purely based on cultural beliefs. Therefore, representatives of different cultures will accuse each other of unethical behaviour.

Power

Cultures have their own way of legitimising the power of their rulers. The British and many other Europeans are hardly impressed by those in authority, and their laws are based on the principle that power should be controlled. This is contrary to cultures in which rulers are given deep respect and great 'freedom of movement', since they provide highly esteemed order and structure in society. In these cultures power is often accompanied by privileges. The most important of these privileges is exemption from the rules that are imposed on others. If the persons in power consider themselves completely above the law, it can be fatal to try to deprive them of their privileges. The Dutch MNC Heineken has been able to successfully challenge this culturally inclined quality of authorities. In several African countries pressure has been exercised on the beer brewer to appoint a relative of the president to a high post within the company. Denying such a favour no doubt leads to a confrontation with the authorities and can be detrimental to the brewery and its labour force. But according such a favour is contradictory to ethical entrepreneurship. Jean-Louis Homé, until July 2002 the African and Middle East Director of Heineken and now retired, took to open conflict with the authorities.

> We apply the same company standards all over the world, so no child labour, reduction of environmental waste, no nepotism. We don't appoint unqualified people. People are supposed to know these company rules. Transparency in the recruitment of your personnel is extremely important. Appointment and promotion at top levels are always decided upon in a dialogue between the country manager and the headquarters in Amsterdam.[2]

Heineken has become quite 'untouchable' by building a structure in which privileges cannot be acknowledged. Of course, it is rather helpful that the brewery is an important economic player in Central African countries.

It is too easy to judge the behaviour of an authority that executes privileges as unethical. To make such a judgement one should first know more about the local culture, about the responsibilities that the authority bears in exchange for these privileges, and about the way the local population estimates this. In many cultures loss of power by the rulers leads to social chaos, regardless of whether the ruler was just or brutal. We've seen this happen over and over again, in Liberia, in Afghanistan and in Iraq.

---

2 All quotes from Jean-Louis Homé are from an interview with the authors, December 2002. Chapter 3 deals extensively with Heineken's experiences in Central Africa.

Organisation

Companies operating in conflict regions will not only be confronted with different political or local aspects of culture but also with differences in organisational culture. Especially when co-operation between several sectors is required, important difficulties can arise between partners if they do not have a sharp eye for the cultural differences in each other's organisations. Currently the profit and not-for-profit sectors often join in the construction of public utilities. Governments of poor countries, especially when they are trying to recover from years of civil war, are eager to have facilities for potable water constructed and run by private companies because they lack the know-how and organisational talent to deliver and maintain these services in a whole region. However, this is a job for which the experience of non-profit organisations (such as women's organisations, farmers' organisations or aid organisations) is beneficial since they know the consumption needs of the local population as well as their economic activities, their cultural habits and their relationships with the local authorities. So, private enterprises tend to work closely together with non-governmental organisations (NGOs). The interests of the private company and the NGO are by and large congruent, but they can also be seriously divergent. A water company, for instance, wants to guarantee a commercial success (the investments have been high), whereas the NGO desires water for all at an affordable rate.

For-profit organisations—the term clearly carries the message—have an organisational culture fit for making profit. If the current culture does not suit that goal, the enterprise will be doomed. Not-for-profit organisations, on the other hand, have a fixed budget, to be spent in a way that pleases sponsors and supporters. If these are not satisfied, the NGO is doomed. These two 'survival strategies' require different organisational cultures with appropriate methods of accountability and communication. Hence, successful co-operation is in no way guaranteed.

Often managers or corporations are not aware of their cultural inclination until they are confronted with people of a different persuasion. Many conflicts stem from culturally defined behaviour: this other person is not acting 'normal'. But behind these judgements are always deep convictions on good and evil, on efficiency and effectiveness—convictions, not reasoned opinions.

International standards

Currently, almost unlimited power is ascribed to MNCs: they represent large capital, are active in countries with failing or almost absent governments, and are only accountable to their shareholders. In order to move them in the direction of more corporate social responsibility and a wider accountability, there is much pressure on them to abide by international standards on human rights, labour conditions and environmental care. By now all international corporations have developed business principles or codes of conduct, but the controversy remains. Most enterprises are strongly opposed to universal codes of conduct with an obligatory character, whereas NGOs consider voluntary codes without independent monitoring as window-dressing or greenwashing.

In this debate on international standards we again see the important role cultural differences play. Former Heineken manager Jean-Louis Homé gives a perfect illustration when he explains his objections:

> Heineken is not in favour of a strict and uniform code of conduct. It is impossible to impose the same way of implementation of a set of values all over the world. We want principles, two or three pages, and then will translate them to the local situation. Corporate social responsibility is a journey, a process. The Anglo-Saxons adore codes of conduct, do's and don'ts, but what is needed is transparency. We have to work out rules that put systems and processes in place. In some countries a conflict can derive from strictly applying the rules and not giving privileges. We accept these things as long as they are transparent and known by everybody. You have dilemmas: sometimes it's grey; it's not in the book. Then you should never decide all by yourself, always involve someone else. Transparency is not the same as public knowledge; it means that the organisation knows.

And, shrugging, he adds: 'Life is sometimes a dilemma.'

Clearly, we hear a Frenchman speaking who has not much affinity with the Anglo-Saxon view. Homé is a typical representative of the Latin cultural notion, which apparently kept him on good terms with Heineken. The *savoir vivre* of many Latin cultures can of course be detected in their management style. Rules are dependent on the context; sometimes it is better to tolerate exceptions than to apply the rules. A particular sense for the situation is highly esteemed, as are creativity and pragmatism. Decisiveness is less important than the quality of the decision. The quality of the decision will not deteriorate if the decision process is taking slightly longer than a snap of the fingers. In Anglo-Saxon countries, however, decisiveness is a highly rated quality. Decisiveness requires ingredients such as plain instructions on what is or is not allowed and ready-made and universally applicable directions.

Process-oriented versus action-oriented

When international corporations in conflict regions are confronted with dilemmas, they will have to consider the cultural differences at stake. They will have a tremendous advantage if they apply some 'cultural intelligence' to the situations they face and the people with whom they have to deal. In our description of the dilemmas in the next five chapters we will give ample attention to cultural differences, especially the four different cultural orientations (see Fig. 2.1) that have appeared to be significant for the MNCs described.[3]

We already quoted Jean-Louis Homé of Heineken, who is of the opinion that corporate social responsibility is a 'process' and not a matter of following prescriptions. He represents a culture with a clear preference for a process orientation of reality, whereas other cultures are what we will call action-oriented. The former doesn't feel the need to give concrete forms to everything. The world is too complicated and unstable. The latter tends to make reality as simple and concrete as possible, tangible, visible and definable. Even evil is concrete (*Economist* 2003): Saddam Hussein and his allies are portrayed with name and rank on a pack of cards, so the worldwide audience understands without effort what happens if 'number 9' is arrested. Rapid decisions and actions fit in such a world: no loitering, get things done. But for process-oriented people, discussion is a central feature, everything is intertwined, all aspects should be

---

3   The concepts of action, process, task and role orientation derive from the cultural model of Mijnd Huijser (2002). Some views are taken from quantitative cultural research by Fons Trompenaars and Charles Hampden-Turner (1998). The differences in organisational culture derive from the works by Kim S. Cameron and Robert E. Quinn (1999).

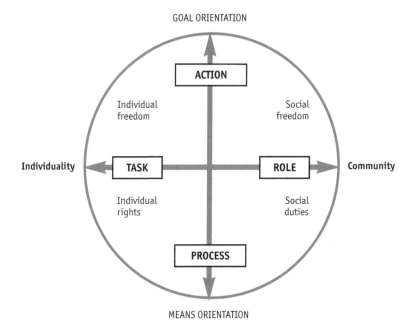

FIGURE 2.1 Four cultural orientations

FIGURE 2.2 All national and organisational cultures fit into one of these four cultural orientations

discussed before action can take place. Process-oriented people are at completely opposite ends of the spectrum from action-oriented people.

A pure demonstration of the action-oriented culture is delivered by Carly Fiorina, former CEO of Hewlett-Packard. When talking about the use of her education in medieval history and philosophy at Stanford University in the US, she explains: 'Every week we had to read a medieval philosophical book and summarise it in two pages. I found it very instructive, this training in finding the essence of a complex whole.'[4] What Fiorina learned was to extract findings that remain valid without the need for a complex context. For process-oriented people this is a torment, since for them there is no meaning without a complex context, covered in thousands of pages of history.

Conceivably, emotions can run high between action- and process-oriented people. Whenever strong convictions are involved, there is a bigger chance that dissidents will be accused. The accusations against action-oriented cultures show a large variety, but all come down to the following: they think in black and white, knowing no shades in grey; matters are settled with a stroke of the pen; they only have an eye for the results; they shoot from the hip. Of course, process-oriented people are accused of the opposite: they talk too much and in the end don't even make very clear decisions; the time they need to aim their weapon could have been used to fire ten rounds—okay, maybe nine misses, but at least one hit.

In action-oriented cultures it is permitted to make mistakes and embark on a new course if that is what the intermediate results indicate. People in these cultures are weary of long preparations and detailed planning; goal setting with short-term targets will do. Process-oriented cultures, on the other hand, will put much energy into avoiding mistakes, because mistakes are considered stupid failures. That is why preparations and planning go into every detail, which, by the way, doesn't necessarily mean that everything goes like clockwork.

Just imagine what happens if the cowboy and the sniper need to co-operate. Each of them will consider the other as incompetent, irresponsible, thoughtless and even unreliable.

4   Interview in *Management Team*, 28 February 2003.

Task-oriented versus role-oriented

> We don't feel responsible for what happens outside of our
> commercial properties. That's where the European Union
> and the United Nations come in. We see to it that in our
> operations no forced labour is applied. We have con-
> tracted a business that closely monitors these matters . . .
> We declined an order for three hoppers, but meanwhile
> China was ever so happy to deliver them to Burma. That's
> how the world is run.[5]

He may sound slightly bitter, but Sjef van Dooremalen, CEO of the
Dutch ship-building company and offshore specialist IHC Caland, has
for many years been 'harassed' by activists for doing business with
the Burmese dictatorship.

Van Dooremalen's attitude should not simply be classified as either
action- or process-oriented. There are two other orientations worth
mentioning: the task-oriented and the role-oriented culture. In task-
oriented cultures, actions and processes are legitimised by the task,
whereas in role-oriented cultures, actions and processes serve to
support the mutual relationships between people. Western MNCs are
mostly task-oriented, regardless of their CEOs' national cultural background. And that is what shows in the attitude of IHC Caland's Dutch
CEO: he is completely assured that he is accomplishing his task in an
appropriate way, and he is irritated by the role orientation of idealistic activists who bother him with matters that he considers beyond
his task.

Task-oriented cultures value the individual, the equality of people
and restricted power for leaders. Everything needs to be functional:
short lines of communication along with clear and direct speech. The
task has the highest priority and there is a strong division between
work and private life. If someone considers his or her rights abused,
there is room for a fierce verbal confrontation, but 'it is nothing
personal' and 'let's not have this disturb our work relationships'. On
the other hand, everything that undermines the fulfilling of the task,
for instance social pressure, is received reluctantly by the entrepreneur: work is work and the job needs to be done.

The task-oriented culture has special difficulties in relating to the
role-oriented culture. Not because role-oriented cultures are not

5   Interview in *Internationale Samenwerking* 4 (April 2003).

focused on their task, but because they choose another way of getting there. Role-oriented cultures do not place much value on individual responsibility in an organisation. Both the individual and the organisation have a role defined by their social context. Their main responsibility is to stick to that role, without questioning why. Deviating ideas about this role are not often appreciated. Belonging to a group is vital in most Asian and African countries: not belonging to a group comes close to being without identity. If everyone sacrifices a little bit of his or her individuality to comply strictly with the role of being a member of a group, this will contribute to the outcome. In role-oriented cultures qualities such as self-discipline, social control, conformist behaviour, formalised communication and avoidance of confrontations are highly valued. Where in task-oriented cultures individual rights are emphasised, role-oriented cultures stress the individual's duties that come with the role. The role behaviour binds individuals together. 'I can keep my role as long as you keep yours, then I know exactly what to expect and how to behave. And thus I feel secure.' There is a shared responsibility for the functioning of the group in relation to the task.

These differences between task- and role-oriented cultures can easily lead to misunderstandings, or even to mutual accusations of unethical behaviour. In Asia and Africa we predominantly find role-oriented cultures. Hence, their companies and institutions have a strongly role-oriented organisational culture. That is why IHC Caland groans at the fact that China takes on an order to build ships for Burma. And that is why the British State Secretary for Development, Clare Short, groaned at the, in her eyes, insufficient anti-corruption programmes of the presidents of Sierra Leone, Malawi or Tanzania. For instance, the fact that the Sierra Leonian president Ahmad Tejan Kabbah fired one of his ministers for stealing diamonds was not considered sufficient for the biggest donor to Sierra Leone to continue its economic assistance programme. But President Kabbah was convinced that he had done exactly what was asked for, considering his role. It suited his role well to fire his fraudulent minister, but he has no place in making personally accountable his civil servants implicated in corruption.

Firmness, so typical of task-oriented cultures, appears ineffective in many Asian and African cultures; it may even be destructive. In role-oriented cultures people are very sensitive to what is needed to keep good relationships going between the persons that accomplish the task.

Role-oriented cultures are less susceptible to international social or political pressure. The strong emphasis on relationships creates group behaviour that excludes members of other groups. Someone who belongs to another group by definition does not have the same rights. That explains why Asian MNCs do not feel compelled to be responsible for foreign social problems, even if they operate in that society for a considerable length of time. Viewed from their cultural context, you can't simply judge that they act unethically.

The four cultural orientations play an important role in the dilemmas faced by Western MNCs in conflict regions. Considering this diversity, it may be obvious that there is no standard recipe for ethical entrepreneurship. The most attractive option for an entrepreneur is, of course, an ethically justified decision that is also economically the most favourable. But such a clear option is not likely to occur in conflict regions; it will have to be created.

3

Enterprise and government

Dilemma: Multinational corporations in conflict regions are compelled to take over public tasks: infrastructure, health-care, education, and sometimes even tax collection. This undermines the already weak position of the government. At the same time, a responsible corporation cannot close its eyes to the social problems in its region of operations.

This is not a very happy array of countries: Rwanda, Democratic Republic of Congo, Burundi. The post-independence history of these Central African states is marked by the bloodshed of coups, inter-ethnic clashes and resource-driven wars between seven, eight or nine national armies. The war in Congo is sometimes even referred to as 'African World War I'.

Nevertheless, the Dutch brewery Heineken has sustained its presence in the region for over 40 years—sometimes to its own amazement. Jean-Louis Homé, until July 2002 the Africa and Middle East Director of Heineken, recounted:

> In the late eighties I started working in Africa. If somebody would have told me then: you will be operating in Rwanda, Burundi and Congo-Kinshasa during wartime, but you will still be profitable, see prosperity and happy people, I would have thought that he was crazy. But it's exactly what has happened.[1]

Heineken is the largest source of income for some African nations. The brewery provides an income for many thousands of employees, and government treasuries are fed with millions and millions of dollars through taxes and shares. The company is showered with

1 All quotes from Jean-Louis Homé are from an interview with the authors, December 2002.

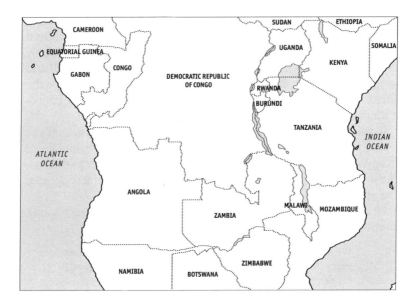

both admiration and criticism: admiration for its 'decent' behaviour and for persisting under difficult circumstances; criticism because the company financially feeds highly disputable regimes that are involved in covert or full-blown civil war.

The roots of the conflicts in Rwanda, Burundi and Congo-Kinshasa are multiple and complex, but one thing on which all peace mediators agree is that economic recovery is a major prerequisite for ending the conflicts. As long as unemployment and exclusion of large parts of the societies linger on, the conflicts will easily find new fuel. As the former Special Representative of the United Nations for Burundi (1993–1995), Ahmedou Ould Abdallah, once stated:

> Poverty is an important cause of most violent conflicts in the world, in Albania, in Afghanistan, in the Great Lakes Region in Africa. The solution is not to further impoverish these countries through embargoes. The situation will improve by staying in the country, by keeping trade alive, by continuing development co-operation, be it under certain conditions.[2]

2 NRC/*Handelsblad*, 20 March 1997.

Former Heineken CEO Homé and the Mauritanian UN diplomat know each other very well. In his Paris apartment Homé takes Ould Abdallah's book *La diplomatie pyromane* from the shelf and proudly shows the author's inscription: 'To Homé, my friend in Burundi and in the Netherlands. In sweet memories of his apprehension for the Great Lake District and to thank Heineken for its excellent contributions to peace in Burundi. January 1997.'[3]

It was Ould Abdallah who strongly objected to pressure on the Dutch brewer to retreat from Burundi in 1997. This pressure came from Western public opinion and Burundian opposition parties because allegedly the brewer's revenues for the Tutsi regime supported the army in carrying out genocide against the Hutus.

Homé, intimately acquainted with operations in conflict regions, sums up the leading principles that he follows: First,

> We are a factor, never a political actor. You are part of the game, but you have to stay a factor. As a brewer we invest for decades, and we have to take care of long-term prosperity. It means you cannot abandon a country just like that. When campaigners ask you to leave, they want to make the government of that country feel uncomfortable, but what they forget is that it is the people who are going to suffer. We never get so strongly involved with a government that we are discredited in the eyes of a newly installed government. In Rwanda, in 1994, we were confronted with the new man in power. He said to me: 'You have supported the previous government.' I said, 'No, I have paid taxes, but I have never supported the government or its policy. So tell me, what did I do wrong?' He then said, 'You gave the previous minister some crates of beer.' I answered, 'I will treat the new minister likewise.' And that was it.

His second principle:

> Take care of your people because they are Heineken people. You are responsible for them in every decision you make. You always have to keep their safety in mind.

---

3   Original inscription: *À Homé, que j'ai connu au Burundi et aux Pays Bas. En souvenir de son amour et de sa connaissance de la région des Grands Lacs, mais également en remerciement de l'excellent travail de Heineken en faveur de la paix au Burundi.*

Referring to the *coup d'état* in Burundi in 1996 and the pressure from Burundian exiles to close the brewery, Jean-Louis Homé asks,

> Would it have been responsible to abandon 1,200 employees? No.

He held on to this position and kept the brewery running.

The third principle Homé follows is:

> Take care not to engage yourself. Stay professional; don't let your own moral judgement prevail. In business you should act according to what fits in with the long-term objectives of the company. It is a prerequisite that you look for profit. I must say that our company policy toward working in conflict regions has changed in the course of time because we have learned from experience. In comparison with 25 years ago, there is now more awareness that we should keep distant from politics. Of course you have your opinions, and in tense situations it is tempting to intervene. That is why country managers are exchanged after a couple of years.

'Our people'

'Our people' is an expression Jean-Louis Homé uses frequently. Heineken people are a large family, and it is a privilege to belong to that family. Heineken wants to take good care of the family. The company has invested in education and training of the local workforce, so it is in Heineken's own interest to see them become healthy and productive employees. Taking good care of 'our people' also means that the production will continue in order to produce an income for the workforce, even in times of violence. Homé adds:

> During the genocide in Rwanda in 1994, we had to stop working for a short while. The question was not *if* we were going to be back but *how*. In Gisenyi we had 300 of the original 900 people left. They were eagerly looking at us, asking, 'Are we going to work again?'

Good care also involves safety. Heineken has taken a wide range of measures to limit the risks. The brewer must see to it that the employees can get safely back and forth to their workplace, so working hours have to be adapted, special transportation has to be arranged, and deliveries in dangerous areas might have to be stalled. 'But,' says Homé,

> safety is not only a physical matter. It also involves re-
> sponsible behaviour of the company. If we operate in
> countries that are dangerous, we have good communica-
> tion guidelines. We have our own radio network every-
> where. Sites are guarded either by the national police, by
> a private agency, or by our own guards. Everyone who
> works on our premises has to abide by our worldwide
> standards. This also goes for the security personnel.

Heineken provides ample healthcare for its people. The company doesn't boast about it; on the contrary. Homé expands:

> Of course we have special community programmes. We
> take care of the people around us. But, how to say this,
> community projects are more a PR thing; they are under-
> taken to be able to say, 'Look, we are good and beautiful.'
> Community projects are not fundamental. If you carry
> out community projects you cross the border between a
> development organisation and a company. We do things
> in terms of charity, but we never disclose them because
> we do not want to use this image of helping poor people.

Widely publicised, however, is Heineken's battle against HIV/AIDS: medicines for both prevention and cure are available for all employ-ees in Africa, including spouses and children. That is not a matter of charity but an indispensable measure to keep the assembly line manned. Heineken is not unique in this matter. Multinational corpo-rations such as Unilever, Coca-Cola and DaimlerChrysler run com-parable programmes, since their productivity is also endangered by the rising mortality of their employees.

Public tasks

Heineken is fully aware of the fact that the company intervenes in the public domain. But what if governments fail in this respect? Homé's view is:

> In Central Africa, in Nigeria or in Ghana the state system
> is not performing as it should. For us, it would be a mere
> fleabite to fulfil some of these public tasks. But we shouldn't
> enter that domain. We draw the line at providing health-
> care for our own workers and their families.

Large enterprises operating in countries with failing public facilities are always under pressure to fill the gap. The population is
impressed by a foreign company that immediately sets itself up by
constructing roads, airports, comfortable homes with swimming
pools and tennis courts for their expatriate staff, water supplies and
brand-new cars. Such a company shows a level of prosperity that is
only a far-off dream for the local population. They consider the
means of the company limitless and of course start demanding their
share. Very often the pressure also comes from the local authorities,
who are eager to see the water and electricity supplies extended to
the surrounding villages.

If companies take over public tasks, they can create a dangerous
situation. The government no longer feels compelled to spend its
budget on healthcare, education, or potable water and thus saves
money for other expenditure (such as tanks or other weapons). Another risk is that the state loses even more of its legitimacy among
the population if it places responsibility for public facilities in the
hands of private companies. And an obvious, but undesirable, result
is that the facilities are limited to part of the population, namely the
employees of a company or its operating area. This inequity can in
itself cause new conflicts.

Homé knows the risks:

> It is in our own interest not to create an oasis of wealth.
> You cannot create a sustainable improvement in the wel-
> fare of your people if the surroundings are in misery. So
> if we develop an HIV clinic, we try to involve other compa-
> nies, and we hope the public sector will join in. The same
> goes for education. For instance, we are now building an
> IT centre. We search for professionals and get them started.
> Later we will retreat into the background. I realise that
> we have to be careful about entering the public domain.
> Many times we have been asked to build primary schools.
> I have always replied that I cannot explain such expenses
> to my shareholders.

Homé's firm belief is that the company should stick to its business.

If we enter the public domain, all the non-governmental organisations will accuse us of putting ourselves in the place of the government, which is not legitimate since we are not a democratically elected body. Sometimes the line between what is business and what is government is very thin, and I've been under enormous pressure to cross that line. But I'm very passionate about it: do not leave your domain.

The company as a cash cow

Jean-Louis Homé's position may appear to be clear and simple, but how should an MNC act if a government foists its responsibility onto them? It has happened to Heineken several times. A striking example that gained much media attention took place in Congo-Kinshasa. In 1997 problems arose. Heineken, Kinshasa's fattest cash cow, decided to raise the price of the beer, in compensation for the high inflation. This led to lower sales and hence to lower tax incomes for the government. The Congolese Minister of Finance called Heineken into his office and demanded a price cut. Upon the brewer's refusal, both the general manager and the controller were jailed. Now the government wanted a lower beer price *and* $1 million in exchange for the release of the Belgian and the Frenchman. Jean-Louis Homé was put in an impossible situation:

> Everybody said that I shouldn't pay, because it would set a precedent. That was a risk, yes, but my people were in jail! My deputy and I contacted everybody: embassies, Brussels, Washington. Giving in to the demands was very controversial. Then I took inspiration from something that, around the same time, was happening in my home country. Jean-Christophe Mitterrand, son of the former president, was put in prison and charged with complicity in illegal arms traffic and abuse of power. But his relatives bailed him out for $700,000. Ah, I thought, what is done in France can also be done in Kinshasa. I offered the government a bail, not a ransom. For $1 million I got my people out of jail and out of the country. Because there was no charge against them, we later got the bail back. Unfortunately it was returned in local currency against the official rate, so we're still trying to get the rest back.

> By the way, I happened to run into this Finance Minister some time later in Prague at a meeting with the IMF, World Bank and African Ministers of Finance. He was completely isolated and he came to me for help to get in touch with people from the Bank. I said, 'Look who you're asking this!'

Governments can really complicate things for companies if they turn to them to compensate for possible deficits in their own budget. According to Homé, a company should always object to such a move and should seek external support.

> It is very hard to deal with an inconsistent financial environment in which a Minister of Finance can come to collect another $10 million whenever he has a deficit. That's why I am in touch with the international financial institutions. There is sometimes a rebound effect between the IMF and local governments. The IMF is right to stress that a country should implement an appropriate system for tax collection before it is eligible for loans. But if the conditionality is, say, 8% of GDP, and by the end of the year the Finance Minister has a deficit, he can come to us, private companies, to ask for more. So we say to the IMF, look, your conditions lead to companies that have to bleed, which makes its economic activity in such a country unattractive. The solution is that the IMF not only sets the conditions but also helps countries to meet them. In that way the private sector is protected.

Inter-ethnic conflicts

Apart from financial demands by the government, MNCs may also be confronted with the government's efforts to influence the recruitment of personnel. This is obviously a very sensitive matter in countries with inter-ethnic conflicts. Haphazardly appointing people from various ethnic groups inevitably brings trouble both on and off the premises.

Big trouble may lie ahead if high-ranking officials appeal for a well-paid job for someone of their own clan. Both consent and refusal can damage the company. Jean-Louis Homé had his fair share of experience with this issue during his term in Central Africa:

Frankly speaking, the pressure on us has been very high. The outcome of our experience is that it is better to have an open conflict and to resist pressure to hire the cousin of the president. Our rules for hiring people are the same all over the world: If someone doesn't qualify, he will not be appointed. Transparency in the recruitment of your personnel is extremely important. We see to it that everybody knows our rules and that everybody knows that we stick to them. Appointment and promotion at the top level are always decided upon in a dialogue between the country manager and the headquarters in Amsterdam.

It is not always possible to avoid importing inter-ethnic conflicts into the brewery. Homé explains:

Inside the company you have behaviour due to the surroundings. We do not try to hide that we have problems in our brewery between ethnic groups. We learned that it is better to bring the conflict into the open. But if you have a conflict in the country that has an impact on your people, be careful not to judge. It's very difficult, but for me it's the outcome of experience. The brewery is not able to fix an outside conflict. If this conflict brings tension into the brewery, you have to stick to the rules of the justice in the country.

We once had a manager who was suddenly jailed because of political reasons. Not only was he put in jail, he also disappeared. He was taken from prison by the military, and it was unknown where he was kept. We were under pressure by the family to do something for him, and after a few days we were also under pressure from the plant manager, who wanted to fire him because he didn't show up at work.

In such situations I always keep in mind how I would react if this was happening in France or the Netherlands. I would act according to the law of the country. Now if there is a charge, and the prisoner is treated well, you cannot intervene in the judicial process. In this case it was unlawful to let the man disappear, so we did everything to find out where he was. We orchestrated a stream of telephone calls from Heineken local and Heineken Amsterdam. We succeeded in tracing him. It was then possible for his family to visit him in jail, and he was treated according to normal legal procedures in the country at that time. He was not 'a disappeared person' anymore. Of course you are tempted to intervene further, but there is a danger of over-reaching if you respond according to your opinions instead of the rules. You can only raise hell if the events are unlawful.

Influencing the government

Supposedly an MNC such as Heineken, being of vital importance for an African country, has the leverage to set conditions for the government and can influence the behaviour of that government during the conflict. But Jean-Louis Homé fiercely contradicts this assumption.

> I think we can only tell the government what conditions would make our business prosper. We have the right to speak on behalf of our interests, but I would never threaten a government to withdraw from the country if it does not behave. If you strongly believe that your presence is beneficial in the long term for the country, and that is my conviction, then you should not leave the country. Look at what is happening in Central Africa. In Congo-Kinshasa the political process was a mess: Mobutu, Kabila the old, Kabila the young. It was a period in which you really wondered what was to become of the country and our operations there. But three years later the situation has changed a little bit, and three years is nothing. I would be very cautious of taking the decision to leave a country because of the regime.

Then how about Burma, a country where Heineken divested after heavy pressure from public opinion? 'That was a totally different matter,' states Homé, 'because the brewery had not yet started operating, so there was no need to fire hundreds of people.'[4]

In some Central African countries Heineken has been asked to participate in peace-building activities. Homé has always refused to do that.

> It is very hard to say no, but you have to. Being a direct actor in peace building is not the vocation of a company. It is so tricky, and I strongly recommend not doing it. If, as an enterprise, you act with decent rules, then you are

4 As a matter of fact, the brewery was later opened by Asia Pacific Breweries from Singapore, an enterprise of which Heineken owns 42.5%.

part of the stabilisation of the country. Ould-Abdallah said to me that Heineken should stay in a country in conflict because it is important to have witnesses. I agree with that. But I do not agree with him if he means we should report what we witness. I said to him: 'No, we are only involved as a factor, not as an actor.'

The division of domains

Even in countries with a well-functioning government, there is not always a sharp distinction between the responsibilities of the government and those of the private sector, and in the course of time the boundaries can be subject to change. Where in many countries the protection of citizens and their possessions has always been a task of the government, one nowadays sees some aspects of this task being privatised. There is also a difference of opinion between Western countries on the range of the government and that of the private sector. In the US, for instance, sponsoring of schools and universities by companies is completely accepted, a development that is in most European countries considered a potential loss of independence in the educational system. The 'division of domains' depends to a great extent on national preferences, inspired by the culture of the country. This becomes all the more complicated in conflict regions in which a government cannot or does not want to take care of its population.

MNCs also have differences in boundaries. Heineken is quite resolute in protecting its 'domain': constructing an HIV clinic is all right, because your workforce diminishes if you do not invest in healthcare. But constructing primary schools? No way! Shell, on the other hand, stretches its boundaries. In 2000 the then CEO Mark Moody-Stuart stated[5] that 'the successful companies will be those who work hardest to make sure that they are in tune with the needs and aspirations of society'. According to Moody-Stuart, that society does not end at the company gates or the office car park.

5 'Putting Principles into Practice: The Ethical Challenge to Global Business', speech by Mark Moody-Stuart, during the World Congress of the International Society of Business, Economics and Ethics, São Paulo, Brazil, 19 July 2000.

> It's our view that good business and sustainable develop-
> ment go hand in hand. This means, for example, improv-
> ing the way that we engage with communities affected by
> our activities to reduce the potential drawbacks of new
> developments and to improve local opportunities.

Thus, Shell expands its 'domain' much further than Heineken. The oil company has established a Sustainable Development Council to see to it that the economic, social and environmental elements of the business principles are integrated in everyday operations. This has nothing to do with charity or money for community projects, Moody-Stuart stresses:

> While community support is important, it is a great mis-
> take to focus on this as the main social contribution that
> companies can make. This approach ignores the far more
> significant social contribution that we can make through
> our core business activity, whether measured in terms of
> employment, payment of taxes, or investment.

Shell is well aware of the fact that the company can enter the government's domain with its social contributions. That is why the oil company does not act any more on its own accord but co-operates with governments, civil-society organisations and sometimes universities. For instance, in Brazil Shell has adopted a ban on child labour in its contracts with distilleries. The alcohol these distilleries supply (to add to gasoline) comes from sugar cane fields, where children usually work. So together with civil-society organisations, local governments and distilleries Shell has found a solution by compensating families for the loss of income from the children. Funds have also been generated to offer education for these children.

Since there are no general criteria for the 'legitimate crossing of boundaries', there is always room for heavy bickering whenever companies enter the public domain. On the one side there is pressure from society on companies to build health centres for the whole region, not exclusively for the employees. On the other side, there is the feeling that public facilities should not be left in the hands of 'the market'. Companies such as the French Ondeo and Vivendi Water, with contracts in developing countries for constructing water facilities, were fiercely targeted by pressure groups when they raised the price of water, whereas most of the clients were used to having free water. But nobody is happy when these companies withdraw from privatised facilities due to lack of profit.[6]

6   A World Bank (2004) study found that credible regulation is essential to

NGOs in Western Europe and the US are vehemently opposed to interference by MNCs in state policies, but at the same time they want companies to use their political contacts, for instance in Latin American countries, to change oppressive practices.

Reconciling the dilemma

Reconciling this dilemma is better than looking for a compromise or making a decisive list of domains belonging to the government or to MNCs. A compromise will not be effective, since there will always be frustrated parties. And a decisive list will not work either, because the situation differs from country to country and from conflict to conflict. It makes a considerable difference whether the government's power is reduced to the capital, being surrounded by rebel forces, or reaches far into the jungle. It matters whether a government is deep into the drugs trade or is as innocent as a newborn baby but also as poor as a church-mouse. It is an illusion to suppose that Western ethical standards are applicable in all of these situations.

It is also obvious that a company will not find a satisfactory way out of the dilemma all on its own. A company simply cannot answer the appeal to be responsible for the prosperity in a region and at the same time stick to its domain.

There is a possible reconciliation process, although it has not often been done and is certainly not accepted worldwide. The solution is that government, MNCs and (international) NGOs act in co-operation. In such a partnership each party contributes its core business: the MNC provides for productivity, capital and organisational capacity, the government delivers a vision or policy and its reliable civil servants (if there are any), and the NGO provides its expertise in community development. If this combination works, there is no end to the advantages. Crossing the boundaries is a responsibility shared

ensure improved performance of utilities such as water, power, transportation and telecommunications. Regulatory agencies must be free of political influence, and their decisions must be subject to review by the judiciary or oversight by another non-political entity. Regulatory processes, it urges, must encourage competition, be open and transparent, and be designed before privatisation is undertaken.

with all the partners, the government is not undermined but controlled, and the provision of community services is not dependent on the presence or absence of a company. True, *if* it works.

Of course in such a collaborative effort between three parties it is crucial to bridge the differences in organisational culture. A for-profit organisation such as an MNC has a decision-making process characterised by clear hierarchy and relatively short communication lines. That can easily collide with the more meandering and bureaucratic procedures of a government that has to keep in mind a diversity of interests. And a non-profit organisation such as an NGO often has a process or role orientation: widely discussing matters, searching for dialogue, finding out what its supporters want, focusing on *how* to get somewhere, not on *what* to get there. It is an orientation that can drive an MNC nuts. In Chapter 7 we will amply highlight the obstacles to such co-operation through the words of the participants.

It will not always be easy or possible to create such a mixed set-up. Sometimes it will be impossible to co-operate with local governments, for instance if they propagate political violence. And it is hard to picture co-operation with a government that considers every NGO a potential enemy. Above that, a task-oriented MNC will find it hard to find access to African and Asian governments that require a long process of showing respect before they open up. Neither will every NGO find it ethically just to partner with an MNC.

But even in the absence of intricate partnerships, the corporate world can do more to find a way out of the dilemma than just avoiding all the risks. For instance, Jean-Louis Homé, now that he is retired, puts a lot of effort into lobbying international organisations such as the EU, the World Bank, IMF and OECD for a consistent and coherent strategy for economic development. It is a double-edged sword. It is more efficient if companies and institutions do not obstruct but help each other, and the mistrust against companies diminishes if they do not act purely on their own accord. Even today, Homé is confronted with that mistrust against enterprises in general and specifically against those operating in conflict regions:

> The risk of operating in developing countries is not so much an issue of finances but of reputation. How can we operate in Congo-Kinshasa without hurting our reputation in the United States? Our problem is not so much the African government but the activist in San Diego.

Much of that mistrust can be removed by better communication with all the local stakeholders: the population in the region of operations, the employees, local and national governments, civil-society organisations and pressure groups. That presupposes that a company has the will to be transparent about its plans and policies. It also presupposes thorough knowledge of local norms and values; if not, parties will not recognise themselves in the communication. It also implies a sophisticated strategy: do not start being transparent about your intentions after hell breaks loose, but adapt a clear communication right from the beginning of the operation. In that way MNCs gain trust and show that they are accountable for the effects of their operations on the society.

Much is also to be gained by improving the communication with stakeholders outside of the operations region. To achieve this, companies will have to study the norms and values of these stakeholders, e.g. international NGOs. If a company in a conflict region wants to engage with an NGO in reducing military influence in a certain region, the NGO will understand that this is not an overnight matter. But this understanding will easily wear off if the company is not clear about the steps it is taking while, in the meantime, illegal blockades by uniformed men continue. If the company puts effort into providing information on its position and in engaging civil-society organisations in the process, it can prevent interpretations that harm the company's image. But this implies that the entrepreneur is not only a competent manager but also a business diplomat.

Heineken tries to follow this line. According to Homé,

> With the help of corporate communication and with outside assistance we worked out a communications plan for each African operation. In each country we have established who our relevant stakeholders are and how we want to communicate with them. We also established what kind of communication we want with the World Bank or the European Union.

This man, with his long-time African experience, is allergic to eurocentrist utterances, even if they sprout from highly ethical principles:

> For African people it is important to be treated with dignity, also from the international community. If the world doesn't accept that we are in Africa to make money, that is ultimate racism. Humiliation and racism! It is important not to feel guilty about operating in Africa. When I

started, I had to appoint a lot of people and had difficulty finding them. When I left, there were many people who were eager to work for Heineken. We just have not yet tackled the matter of public opinion.

4

Clean hands and failing states

Dilemma: It is ethically just to invest in failing states, because raising prosperity contributes to stability. However, it is also ethically just if companies stay out of these countries. But in neither situation does a company keep its hands clean. When investing, a repressive regime benefits from joint ventures and tax levy. But divesting largely hits the poor population, while the leaders are not personally affected.

We have signed a contract with the state of Myanmar, not with 'the government'. When signing a contract, you don't know who is in the government after 10 years, when revenue starts to flow, let alone who will benefit from that contract after 20, 30 or 40 years.

Olivier de Langavant, CEO Myanmar[1] of Total, is a friendly man in his forties. He appears almost light-hearted, although he faces agonising problems. During his previous assignment, Angola, Total faced heavy scrutiny because the local government financed its war against the rebel movement with income from oil (Global Witness 1999). And here in Burma the French energy giant has to defend itself constantly against two accusations: first, of having used forced labour in building the pipeline; and, second, of sustaining the military junta.

In his office, delightfully located on the edge of a lake in the north of the Burmese capital, a special drawer is reserved for *'politically related matters'*. 'It belonged to my predecessor,' De Langavant

---

1 The interviewees prefer using the official names of country and capital: Myanmar and Yangon. In the West the old names Burma and Rangoon are still current.

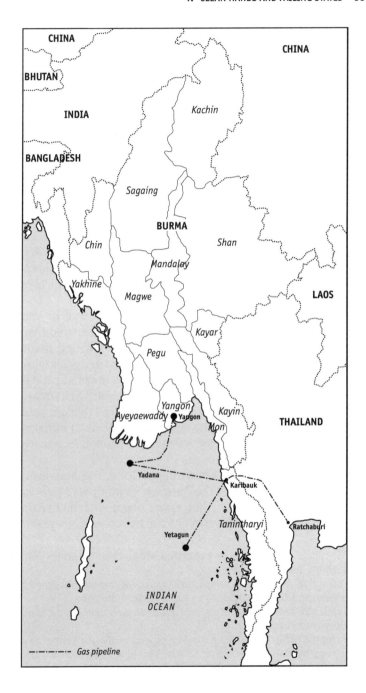

grins.[2] 'I have not yet looked into it.' It sounds cool, but at the end of the interview he admits being 'heavily frustrated by the constant accusations from international campaigners. There are so many outstanding things done in Myanmar. We haven't had a good communication strategy.'

Burma is, to put it mildly, a problematic country. The government, which introduced the pre-colonial name Myanmar in 1989, is struggling to prevent the country from disintegrating, and in doing so it violates all basic human rights. Ever since independence ethnic groups have fought for secession. The country has become an international pariah because of the repressive military regime. The US, Canada and the EU have tried to correct the regime by means of economic and political sanctions. To begin with, the junta needs to respect the results of the 1990 elections, won by the National League for Democracy (NLD). Figurehead of the NLD, Aung San Suu Kyi, was placed under house arrest long before the elections were held. She was released in 1995, but whenever she undertakes political activities, her freedom of movement is again restricted.

Doing business with Burma is highly controversial in Western public opinion. Aung San Suu Kyi has repeatedly declared that economic co-operation with Burma is fundamentally wrong, because it means legitimising a reprehensible regime. Total disagrees with 'The Lady'. According to Total, putting a country on the blacklist will not lead to economic, social and political development.[3] In its CSR report in 2003[4] the company declared: 'We are convinced that our presence benefits the country's economy and that our societal initiatives in our host region help to create sustainable economic activity and promote human rights.'

Since 1992 a consortium consisting of Total, the American firm UNOCAL, the Thai PTT EP and the Burmese counterpart Myanmar Oil and Gas Enterprise (MOGE) has spent about $1.2 billion on the Yadana gas project,[5] an investment for the coming 30 years. The

2 All quotes from Olivier de Langavant are from an interview with the authors, February 2003.
3 *Yadana: An Industrial Development Project in Myanmar*, published by the consortium Total, UNOCAL, PTT EP and MOGE, June 2002.
4 Total: CSR report 2003, *Myanmar: Promoting Human Development in a Heavily-Criticized Country*.
5 From the offshore Yadana gasfield a pipeline runs 364 km to the coast. It runs overland from Daminseik to Thailand, a further 60 km. The pipeline provides energy for two Thai electricity plants.

difficulty is in the construction of the pipeline. People in the area say that the military has forced them to work. Total keeps denying this. Olivier de Langavant understands what has fed the accusations:

> Long before we signed the contract, the pipeline was designed to be built in an area where heavy fighting between the army and the rebels had been going on. Complete villages have been evacuated; the population was forced to leave. In that region a railway has been constructed by means of forced labour. Some of the labourers fled to Thailand and do not want to return to Myanmar. They have an interest in telling how bad the situation in Myanmar is. There is a lot of confusion, because it is even more complicated. When we signed the contract in 1992, the pipeline was to be built in that conflict zone. In 1995 we decided, for various reasons, to plan the pipeline about 200 km more to the south. But by that time we were already implicated in displacing villages, which, of course, has never been the case!

Dialogue

According to independent researchers, who visited the area of the pipeline three times in the period between October 2002 and December 2003, the local inhabitants feel protected against forced labour by the presence of foreign oil companies.[6] In the villages in Total's operations area, the inhabitants told the researchers that it was years and years ago that they experienced forced labour. Whenever the military made such an attempt, they warned Total, who took up the matter with the government.[7]

What the case of Total makes very clear is that a company will always be contaminated by the ongoing conflict in its area, regardless of whether the company has an easy or a heavy conscience. Even if Total's conduct is spotless, the company will be bombarded with accusations till the end of time. The stain on its reputation is not removed by the fact that the company creates employment, trains

6 Corporate Engagement Project, reports of field visits, www.cdainc.com.
7 In Burma some types of labour are obligatory but are not considered 'forced labour', such as cleaning a pagoda or repairing a road after heavy rains.

people to be highly skilled technicians, provides healthcare for 45,000 inhabitants, and protects them against the arbitrariness of the military in the area. That is because the second accusation is that Total sustains the junta since the Burmese government earns a large income from the pipeline. That was hardly the case between 1992 and 2001, when the Burmese counterpart MOGE (with a 15% share) had to invest too. But, starting in 2005–2006, the pipeline will bring in a considerable amount of money to the state treasury, and that is a welcome boost for a government ruling a country that is in a deplorable condition. Unfortunately it is not likely that the state will use its income to invest in healthcare, education or employment since the government's priority is to reinforce the army in order to have 'order and calmness' reign in every region of the country.

So the question arises whether the Total consortium has made agreements with the Burmese leadership about budget spending or whether the company awaits a 'Burma-gate', much the same as when it previously faced an 'Angola-gate'. No, there are no agreements with the leaders. The company is of the opinion that it cannot get involved in politics, since it is not a democratically elected body. But there is 'dialogue'. Olivier de Langavant states:

> Campaigners keep insisting that we are in a position to influence government officials because we are an important player. We do that. As soon as we came into the country, we spoke with the government about the practice of forced labour, and we got support from the authorities to end forced labour in our area right from the start. Since 1999 we can also use as a leverage the official order that now prohibits that practice.[8] If the army tries to use forced labour, we stop it with the support of our Myanmar counterpart MOGE. Attempts very seldom occur nowadays, and it is always possible to stop them right away. Our usual counterpart is the Minister of Energy. We tell him, 'We are in a bad situation. We are constantly confronted with false accusations of forced labour because you do not end that practice. So you have to do something.'

Total says that it works within the existing laws and regulations of a country, wherever it is in the world. De Langavant explains:

---

8   The International Labour Organisation (ILO) puts heavy pressure on the government to inspect observance of the order, but not to much avail.

> It is a mistake to think that it is the task of a company to correct the government on matters such as human rights. What I personally do is tell the government—very carefully, because it is highly sensitive—about human rights because I feel it as my duty as a human being to prevent violations of human rights. We do have the ability to discuss things with the members of the government. Here in Myanmar, in this very special situation, we try to underline to them the importance of democracy. In general a company should not interfere with the opposition to help topple the government or vice versa. In Angola the UN put pressure on us to bring government and opposition together. But what legitimacy do we have? I think that is the role of the UN or of elected bodies. In Myanmar you may be tempted to see things as black and white, and you may start to interfere. But we shouldn't help one against the other, as a principle. The only thing we can do is foster a dialogue with the government.

Although the company wishes to maintain its neutrality, it did comment officially on the arrest of Aung San Suu Kyi in May 2003 as it later voiced its interest in the 'road map for democracy', stating that Total wished to see the process launched rapidly, with the participation of all political parties.

Stay or leave

Although Total has been persistently criticised by campaigners for unethical behaviour, since the company is doing business with a regime that abuses human rights, it has decided to stay in the country. Total is convinced that it can do more good by staying than by leaving. How the energy company is going to ward off the attacks on its reputation remains to be seen.

A company that made a different choice is Triumph, the Swiss producer of women's underwear. In 2002 campaigners worldwide represented Triumph's presence in Burma with posters of women wearing bras made of barbed wire. Subsequently, Triumph closed down its factory in Rangoon. It is still not quite clear whether this decision was purely inspired by fear of brand damage or if the sudden changes in tax levy by the government laid such a heavy burden on the firm that it was forced to divest. Triumph's decision was widely deplored in Burma. Its 2,000 employees, the majority being young women, were fired. Triumph had been one of the very few employers that provided an air-conditioned workplace and paid a decent wage. The only beneficiary of the exit of Triumph was a Korean textile firm that has a bad reputation for the way it treats its personnel and for calling in the army whenever labour troubles arise. Because Asian companies seldom show any transparency in their operations, they are less vulnerable to criticism by international campaigners.

At the time of our visit in the spring of 2003, the British energy company Premier Oil was also on the verge of leaving Burma. Its share (more than a quarter) in the Yetagun gas project had been sold to the Malaysian company Petronas, already a partner in the consortium. Ron Aston,[9] who remained in the country for another couple of months as Premier Oil's Burma manager, denies that the company's retreat had something to do with pressure from the British and American governments. He states that the reason for leaving the country is purely a corporate reorganisation. The campaigners behind the flood of criticism aimed at Premier Oil for years on end were triumphant at the exit of the British firm, representing it in the media as their success. Ron Aston notes:

> Campaigners would use the instance of our withdrawal to further their own voice, but you really have to go beyond that. Premier Oil has been in Myanmar for 13 years and has not buckled under any external pressure, not even in darker times, when Aung San Suu Kyi was under house arrest. Sadly enough, we are pulling out of Myanmar completely. After everything we have put in, it is a great shame. We weathered the storm, we have a view, but economic and corporate needs made it necessary to restructure.

Aston sees no political reasons for Premier Oil to withdraw and has no confidence in the strategy of isolating the regime.

> The British government, the US, the European Union, they all believe that a corporate presence in Myanmar validates and supports the military government. The idea is that isolating (no investment, no aid) the country will ultimately lead to the collapse of the regime and to a return to the outcome of the 1990 elections. But the

9   All quotes from Ron Aston are from an interview with the authors, February 2003.

government here has been in place for 40 years, and there is little evidence that it has been persuaded by the Western countries to take a different stand. Also, there is a lot of investment from Asian countries, so the boycott has no effect.

Just like Total, Premier Oil prefers *constructive engagement*, constructive co-operation with the government. Ron Aston expands:

> You don't get anywhere if you don't talk, so we want to engage with the government, keep the dialogue open. Hence, we've been working with them on human rights. Together with the Australian government we hold workshops; Japan will also do so in the future. Gradually, we believe, this is leading to a different view. I meet directly with the Minister of Interior Affairs because of the Commission for Human Rights. They administer workshops that we support financially to bring in internationally recognised experts. Participants are civil servants and policemen. The minister and I have very open discussions on the future of this participation. UN organisations and non-governmental organisations mention to us that corporations should use their influence in a wider sphere. We're all finding our way in how to use or expand our influence. We've tried to do it step by step. In the Asian context, obtaining trust is a slow thing. You can't ignore the political landscape. At the same time, you have a responsibility to ensure that in the direct area where you work nothing happens that interferes with your own code of conduct.

Premier Oil used to run an intricate and large programme for socioeconomic development in its area of operations, providing healthcare, vocational training, micro-credits, environmental projects and courses on human rights for police and military. Part of this development programme was contracted out to the NGO Save the Children US, and Premier Oil hired independent experts each year to evaluate the impact of the programme. When Premier Oil left the country in 2003, Petronas promised to continue the programme for at least two years.[10]

The country managers of Premier Oil and Total are convinced that their presence in the country has an 'educational' impact if they

10 Alexander Tarnoff, Myanmar office of Save the Children, 18 August 2004.

succeed in arranging for the local population to benefit from their economic activities and at the same time influencing the regime. But any economic activity in Burma is widely viewed as 'getting one's hands dirty', which is regrettable.

Premier Oil and Total have been facing the same decision as countless other MNCs: stay or leave? Companies such as Alcatel, Glaxo-SmithKline, Agfa-Gevaert, Compaq, Nestlé and DHL have stayed. But, among others, Shell, Heineken, Carlsberg, Interbrew, Philips and Eastman-Kodak have left. Heineken yielded to the threat of a consumer boycott in 1996, although the company had for years defended its plans for a brewery in Burma, saying it 'was hoping for a positive impact on the Burmese regime'. The same consideration was mentioned by the Belgian pharmaceutical enterprise Usine Chimique Belge (UCB): economic co-operation would force the regime to respect human rights and become more inclined to social development. For UCB it was a reason to stay and continue selling medicines through its Swiss subsidiary, Farchim.

Stalemate

The dilemma of MNCs in Burma is that both staying and leaving can be conceived as ethically justifiable, but both carry negative consequences. By staying they cannot keep their hands clean, because they are committed to a faulty regime. By leaving they promote the isolation of a country, which deprives the population of jobs, knowledge and technology.

It is in nobody's interest to prolong this stalemate. Both in the West and in Asia political leaders, diplomats, multilateral institutions and civil-society organisations are looking for a way out. The moral stance that dictates 'no trade with criminals' succeeded in isolating the Burmese regime but never totally drained its economy. The state's treasury receives income from illegal activities such as the drug trade, logging and uncontrolled border trade. The government, humiliated by its treatment as an international outcast, retreats into impenetrable complacency. Exchanges between intellectuals are scarce because they are easily interpreted as directed against the state. A strong middle class is absent. Again a new generation of students finds the universities closed for a good part of the season. The

Buddhist population accepts its fate, as true Buddhists do, left with no other aspiration than finding food for another day. Meanwhile the country lapses further behind its neighbouring countries such as Thailand, Singapore and Malaysia.

If the assumption is correct that ethical entrepreneurs can play a stabilising role in a conflict region, it is relevant to try to find a way in which the unethical consequences of doing business in Burma can be removed. This requires a clearer understanding of the actions of the government and its adversaries and of the Asian norms and values on which they are based.

First prosperity, then democracy

In February 2002, U Win Aung, the Burmese Foreign Secretary, provided a taste of the way his government is thinking. In the state-owned newspaper, *The New Light of Myanmar*, he wrote:

> For us, the matter concerning democracy is not a problem
> . . . What is most important is to maintain democracy
> after reaching the democratic goal, to prevent misuse of
> democracy and to protect the Union against those who
> try to put it in jeopardy under the pretext of democracy.
> As the leaders of the State have comprehensive visions,
> they have already taken account of all these things. The
> leaders of the State, knowing that if poverty cannot be
> eliminated, it will be difficult to maintain democracy, are
> striving for the emergence of a prosperous, modern and
> developed nation.

He finds support for his statement in Argentina (sweetheart of the West, as he recollects bitterly), where he sees economic decline threatening the stability of the country. Interestingly enough, he also points at Indonesia, the country that for years had served as an example for the junta. Burma has even tried to copy the Indonesian constitution, in which the army has both a military and a political function. But now that Indonesia has a civilian for a president, and political and social unrest is on the rise, the big brother has fallen off his pedestal, as U Win Aung writes: 'Indonesia is also a democracy. The government came to power through election. But, Aceh Province, Irian Jaya Province and Sulawesi Province are not in a stable condition. Even in Jakarta, the situation is not stable.'

The Burmese government is deeply concerned about such unrest in its own territory. And chances are that this may occur in Burma, the union of seven states, where a manifold of ethnic minorities is striving for independence.[11] A widespread military intelligence system, severe restrictions on relations between the Burmese and foreigners, a tight control on civil servants and detention of political adversaries are all means exercised by the government to maintain order and national unity. Half of the budget is spent on defence and the government employs an army of 300,000 men.

Deeply anchored in Asian culture is the concept of favouring economic development above the introduction of democracy. Kishore Mahbubani, the Singaporean ambassador to the United Nations, wrote: 'The first challenge in the development of every society is economic' (Mahbubani 2002). Only after having achieved some prosperity can the government permit freedom that leads to further development instead of disintegration. (This principle has been demonstrated by China, Taiwan and South Korea.) This does not mean that Asians value freedom less than do Westerners. On the contrary, for both Asians and Westerners freedom is of the highest value. But they differ in what is really meant by the word 'freedom'. In Asian countries, with a strongly role-oriented culture and a low need to act separate from the group, people enjoy freedom when they are able to live in security and to share responsibilities. Westerners consider freedom as the possibility to manifest themselves as individuals, who can freely speak their thoughts and can move around as they like. This type of freedom is even more important than food, shelter or education. The Western concept of freedom is not to be free *from* threats but to be free *to* arrange one's life according to one's personal views.[12]

This explains why, for instance, the Americans demand that the Burmese junta give individual and political freedom, under penalty of a boycott. In their view freedom, preferably tailored after Western democracy, ranks above prosperity. Remarkably enough, opposition leader Aung San Suu Kyi, educated in the West, shares this view. She

11 Independence was promised to certain minorities in the constitution of 1947, written under the supervision of General Aung San, Suu Kyi's father.
12 Kishore Mahbubani demonstrated this notion when he slated the *New York Times* for criticising the lack of freedom in Singapore. In this Asian metropolis, countered Mahbubani, the streets are safe in the middle of the night, whereas New Yorkers must fear for their lives at such an hour.

fights for freedom of expression and for democracy, values that in the short run are only important to a relatively small group of Burmese; the rest of the population just wants to improve its standards of living.[13]

Minding your own business

Asian values still show strong traces deriving from an old doctrine—Confucianism. Confucius taught about the virtues necessary to sustain and regulate a society. The binding forces in such a society were the 'true ways' of relationships between family members, between friends, and between rulers and citizens. To behave in 'the right way' was described as a virtue, without which society would break down. Confucius and his disciples thus stressed, through many ages, the importance of role behaviour and helped build role-oriented cultures.

The prototype of the Confucian society was the family; all described virtues were only valid within that family, to be extended to friends only. For many Asians it is still important to identify with a family-type group. Such a group can of course be the family, but it can also be the company, colleagues, friends or fellow countrymen. The Confucian emphasis on identifying with your group makes this group more important to you than other groups, to the extent that other groups have no importance at all. All rules apply only to your own group. The others are not your concern; you mind your own business. Likewise, a state shall never intervene in the internal matters of another state, and this is directly reflected in the way Asian countries deal with Burma. It is perfectly all right for them to establish economic ties with this country, even though they find many deeds of the rulers despicable. China, for instance, has for years been a close ally, delivering weapons and money for infrastructure to the junta.

13   This is not to say that Suu Kyi's attitude is purely Western. It is typically Asian that she keeps up a dialogue with people with whom she disagrees completely, not only members of the junta, but also foreign companies in Burma, such as UNOCAL.

Japan[14] shows at appropriate times a cautious disapproval of the Burmese regime, but above all it tries to work on reciprocal respect and recognition. The Japanese envisage development projects as a possibility to open up the regime and at the same time enhance prosperity. That is why they hold workshops each year for delegations of high-ranking officials from both countries, a way of 'giving face' to the Burmese government by granting the status of a partner in discussions. They choose the development projects in such a way that they are significant for both the men in power (a shiny new airport) and for the population (roads, transportation and energy). Western lobby groups often scold the Japanese for their attitude, but they ignore the fact that Japan belongs to the group of Asian countries that is convinced that economic prosperity is necessary before individual freedom can be granted. Japan respects the right of Burma to be treated according to its own cultural values and approaches Burma in 'the Confucian way'.

In 1997 the Association of South-East Asian Nations (ASEAN)[15] welcomed Burma into the family, very much against the will of the West. But by ASEAN's judgement the attitude of Western countries is paternalistic because they prescribe the way Asians should get along with their neighbours. This is seen as a disgusting display of ethical colonialism. According to ASEAN, Burma should be recognised through engaging in dialogue, a precondition to gradually determine what will be the next step.

In November 2003 the leaders of Cambodia, Laos, Burma and Thailand decided to co-operate in the reduction of poverty. Their fields of co-operation are: trade and investments, agriculture and industry, transportation, tourism and capacity building. A ten-year plan provides for some 40 projects. Again, a proof of the Asian approach: show respect to the leaders and slowly pursue a different path without interfering in each other's internal affairs.

The Burmese junta finds a justification of its actions in Buddhism. Members of the junta say that they live and work according to Buddha's doctrine, just like the Thai or the Chinese. The regime cherishes Buddhism by spending much money on renovation and building of shrines. It pays off because Buddhism, calling for

14 Japan is Burma's largest donor, in 2001 providing more than $80 million, partly in loans.
15 ASEAN members are Indonesia, Thailand, Malaysia, Singapore, the Philippines, Vietnam, Laos, Brunei, Cambodia and Burma.

acceptance of fate, has a calming impact on its followers. In Buddhism the head of the family is accepted if he is just, meaning that he strictly adheres to his role—just as in Confucianism. The same goes for the government as head of the nation, whose role it is to keep the family together. In this fashion Aung San Suu Kyi is seen as a disobedient younger daughter, who nevertheless is treated benignly. In the eyes of the junta the restrictions put on her are merely mild corrective measures, given the danger she represents to the stability of the country. This may partly be due to the fact that her father is still highly respected—his portraits hang on the walls in many official buildings. His fame still lingers around his daughter, a phenomenon also found in other Asian countries such as India (the Gandhi dynasty), Pakistan (the Bhuttos) and Indonesia (the Sukarnos).

Apart from these Buddhist/Confucian values, Burma also has local traditions such as a strong sense of community. For a long time villages have furnished unpaid labour for tasks that are in the interest of the community, such as constructing roads. The regime misuses this tradition for its own good. Many Burmese protest against the duration and the type of work that has been imposed on them but not against the broadly accepted principle of doing unpaid work for their own community.

A vision of half a century

The opinion that an MNC should not do any business with a country where human rights are being violated is starting to erode since apparently this strategy does not have any impact on the regime. China, Iran and Burma are all examples.

The International Labour Organisation (ILO) has a representative in Rangoon, Mrs Hông-Trang Perret-Nguyen, technical adviser to the government.[16] 'They are not happy with me because I am forced upon them,' she says in the office building crowded with UN organisations in the capital. 'But they accept me as a person. Maybe

---

16   Quotes from Mrs Hông-Trang Perret-Nguyen are from an interview with the authors, February 2003. She completed her appointment at the end of November 2003. Mr Richard Horsey was appointed Liaison Officer *ad interim* from 1 December 2003.

because I am Vietnamese and I have had a long career at the ILO.' Her job is to help the government eliminate forced labour. Mrs Perret-Nguyen says

> Isolation of the regime does not help the ordinary people. They remain locked up since they are not confronted with other ideas.

She does notice the dilemma of MNCs, but, she says, 'This country needs investments and aid. Large companies should operate with care, but they could bring positive changes if they abide by their own codes of conduct.' In her view, the presence of MNCs in Burma is most welcome if they arrange for technological innovation and vocational training and if they set a standard for ethical entrepreneurship.

Although Mrs Perret-Nguyen is not in favour of sanctions and isolation, she does advocate putting pressure on the junta to put an end to forced labour:

> The ILO keeps threatening that we will call on governments, labour, employers and international organisations to revise their relationships with Burma. Until now I have not seen enough improvements, but it is a process.

The Burmese businessmen we have interviewed were also in favour of opening up the country by letting in Western companies. One of them is Bernard Pe-Win, a 62-year-old businessman who has spent many years in Great Britain and Hong Kong. But his attachment to his homeland remains so strong that he has tried to save the number one piece of colonial heritage, the famous Strand Hotel on the bank of the Irrawaddy River in Rangoon. He has put up millions of dollars to restore the grandeur of the building, but it is not a commercial success. The very few tourists who show up in this God-forsaken country cannot afford $400 a night for a room; only the coffee shop is a popular meeting place for diplomats. Bernard Pe-Win is also the driving force behind the Business Forum, a kind of social club where businessmen, diplomats and politicians can gather. 'No, nobody from the opposition,' he says, apologising, 'zero tolerance.'[17] What he means is that his club would inevitably be closed down if he gave the floor to dissidents. In the Business Forum villa one can sink in the English armchairs, away from the heat and

---

17   Quotes from Bernard Pe-Win are from an interview with the authors, February 2003.

exhaust fumes, and served by an impeccable waiter. The bookcase offers all the works that are forbidden by the regime. It is hardly unpleasant to wait here a while for Pe-Win to take leave of his lunch partners.

Pe-Win tries to bridge the gap between the junta and the international community, because he is in very low spirits about Burma's isolation:

> What does the military know about development? In 25 years the military has reduced this formerly rich country to one of the least developed countries. They solely invested in the army. There are no good civil servants any more because they cannot work under the military. The army is the only institution that is functioning. It will take decades to rebuild the institutions in Myanmar.

Mentally Bernard Pe-Win commutes between the Western and the Asian range of ideas.

> The West is impatient. American businessmen live from one quarter to the next. At the other extreme of the spectrum is China, where the business world has a vision of half a century. Western politicians are also impatient; they want to see fast results or else they will start threatening punishment. It would be much more effective if the West would say to this government, 'We are interested in the stability of your country. Is there anything we can help you with?' In following this strategy the West should closely watch the local way of solving problems. That could consist of inviting Japan, Aung San Suu Kyi and members of the government for a discussion.

Pe-Win's advice to generate change is a complete unsealing of the country: 'Bring in a lot of humanitarian aid through the UN and aid organisations, boost trade and investment, and start diplomatic ties with the government.'

Reconciling the dilemma

In the eyes of the West it is unethical to co-operate with members of a reprehensible regime. But, from the Asian point of view, one has the right to speak up only if one belongs to 'the family'. That implies that some kind of co-operation with the government is a precondition when striving for ethically just results. Why, then, not explore the manner in which the potential of MNCs can be used for opening up the country and not for further repression of the population?

No individual company has the legitimacy or the power to accomplish this on its own. In the Asian context, the only option is to create a platform by which the regime can be 'persuaded' to change. (This, by the way, does not exclude the kind of coercion about which the ILO representative was talking.) Such a platform should have a broad composition: UN organisations, aid organisations, the government and the private sector.[18] For this platform to succeed, the antagonism between those who appeal for sanctions and those who prefer engagement will have to end. Sanctions have merely delivered moral support to the opposition but have not had any lasting effect other than economic stagnation and a suffering population. And neither has the policy of 'engagement' by Asian countries been able to change the hard-core line of the military junta. A joint strategy would be much more effective than the present one. Such an internationally accepted framework would also give the necessary legitimacy to Western MNCs to start operating in Burma.

A condition for success, however, is a neutral atmosphere. Parties will have to refrain from rhetoric, prejudice and abusive language. Mud-slinging matches, in which the West speaks of 'the paranoid military junta' and 'the Burmese gulag' while the Burmese leaders rail at foreign adversaries in terms of 'eagles and serpents who are hiding behind bushes to catch their prey',[19] will have to be abolished. Of course that will take some time, since Rangoon believes in a Western conspiracy to starve Burma so the population will cry for help and will ask the West to install a friendly government headed by 'the puppet' Aung San Suu Kyi. In that way, the accusation goes, the West would acquire a strategic position in Southeast Asia as a counterweight to the two most densely populated countries in the world, India and China.

18   A comparable effort was applied in Cambodia during the UN peace operation in the early 1990s. It did not work out perfectly, but the post-war reconstruction has developed with an impressive speed, considering the long history of isolation, poverty and assassination of political opponents.

19   The Burmese Foreign Secretary, in the previously mentioned article in *The New Light of Myanmar*, February 2002.

The renowned International Crisis Group (2004) has strongly pleaded with all parties to let go of their antagonism and adopt a new strategy. The independent think-tank, based in Brussels but with regional offices all over the world, asks for the whole international community to 'rethink its basic objectives for Myanmar, balancing what is desirable against what is realistically achievable'. This means, among other things, a recognition that the 1990 election result will not be implemented and that constitutional reform is going to be a gradual process. Benchmarks for change need to be identified but used in a constructive way: lift sanctions as the government makes visible progress and offer incentives for the resumption of international lending and other economic development support measures. And the international community should support, without preconditions, conflict prevention and resolution, institution-building, planning for economic development, and, above all, humanitarian aid for vulnerable groups. The ICG also states that ASEAN has a particular and urgent responsibility to encourage the necessary change, as Burma is supposed to take the ASEAN chair in 2006.

MNCs could play a distinctive role in an international setting whereby all participating parties are accountable for their decisions and the resulting impact. Of course their operations should be impeccable, in the sense that they abide by all international regulations on human rights, labour rights and environmental protection. But their commitment could be extended to influencing the policy of the government and opening up to independent monitoring. Both Premier Oil and Total cautiously enter these domains, but they could be much more effective if they would operate within a broad platform.

Of course, also in such a platform there remains an imperative for MNCs to communicate intelligently about their local decisions. Even if they are convinced that their decisions are ethically justifiable, there will always remain lobby groups who target individual companies for any evil they perceive. It is an illusion to think that companies will succeed completely in staving off the threat of damage to their reputation. But that is not the real danger to an MNC. The real danger lies in local operations that do no fit in with the values and expectations of that society.

5
Power and privilege

Dilemma: Ethical entrepreneurs are right to avoid countries in which they have to make use of undemocratic power structures. But it is also ethically justifiable to engage in business in these countries with the aim of contributing to the development of a war-torn region and to be pragmatic in relation to the present power structures.

The grand-sounding name, Kabul International Airport, conceals the fact that the strip is as broken-winged as Afghanistan itself. Strewn with helicopter wrecks, UN airplanes, men in hard-to-identify uniforms and bodyguards looking important, the scene is typical for a country taken under the wing of the international community, as previously were Cambodia and East Timor. Afghanistan, having almost bled to death after decades of combat, is heavily dependent on external support. After the ousting of the Taliban at the end of 2001 it was mainly International Security and Assistance Force (ISAF) military, aid workers and diplomats who landed at the destroyed airport. Nowadays businessmen also descend, warmly welcomed by the Karzai administration, who long to see the private sector flourish.

The luggage of the men and women arriving in Kabul contains not only toothbrushes and heavy reports but also bundles of money. Afghanistan is a 'cash country', as the banking system has not yet got back onto its feet. Even the government pays its civil servants all over the country through money changers. The Hawala system, known in many Islamic countries, is also common in Afghanistan. It works very simply: you bring your money to a money changer, who sees to it that the beneficiary can collect it with a certain code at another money changer. No need for banks and no need for money transports. Quite efficient, but the system has a poor reputation since

terrorist groups are known to use it for untraceable transactions. Companies using the Hawala system risk being put on the blacklist by the US.

In the future the Hawala system in Afghanistan will certainly encounter competition. In autumn 2003 the interim government of Hamid Karzai granted a licence to a few commercial banks. For the time being they will only open for business in the capital, aiming mainly at foreign clients, so the money changers with their packs of banknotes will not disappear from the streets overnight. Among the new banks is the 'Afghanistan International Bank, in association with ING'. As one of three foreign banks, ING is taking a chance by starting a business in Afghanistan.[1] Arno van Dijken, Director of Institutional and Government Advisory at ING, is quite satisfied.[2] He has conducted the preparation phase, which was a protracted and laborious affair because plans and partners changed constantly. But in September 2003 the licence for a real commercial bank was finalised. ING will deliver the management of the bank. Shareholders are the Asian Development Bank (25%) and three Afghan investors, 'people who have successfully established businesses in the US and the Middle East,' says Van Dijken.[3]

'Development co-operation'

The Afghanistan International Bank (AIB) officially opened in July 2004 with a capital of $10 million. It offers what any commercial bank normally offers: payment services, cashier services, transfers, cheques, loans, credits, guarantees, bid bonds and performance bonds, project financing, etc. Four ING employees are on the AIB's payroll: the CEO, the COO, the head of IT and an econometrist. The other 27 employees are Afghans from the diaspora community, of whom five are women. Locally there were no Afghans available who were able to work in an international surrounding, according to ING.
Arno Van Dijken explains:

> At the moment about 30% of the money for Afghanistan really comes into the country. The rest remains in bank accounts abroad. Now that our bank is in operation, I expect more donor money to enter the country, maybe up to 50%. In the beginning we will focus on large investors, foreign companies, multilateral organisations, embassies, aid organisations and ISAF. By July 2004 we had opened some 100 accounts.

And the AIB has immediately started rebuilding the financial infrastructure. The Dutch CEO of the AIB will become the first chairman of

1   The other two are Standard Chartered Bank and the National Bank of Pakistan. Also starting operations was the First Microfinance Bank, an initiative of the Aga Khan Foundation.
2   All quotes from Arno van Dijken are from interviews with the authors, September 2003 and June 2004.
3   ING is not a shareholder.

the national association of banks, an institute that will regulate the banking system in Afghanistan. Six local and three international banks will be associated. Van Dijken adds, 'We expect to play an educative role in the country.'

ING considers its involvement in the AIB as a kind of development co-operation. The first couple of years will not be profitable, but of course ING's involvement is not pure altruism. Apart from the fact that they have some personnel on the payroll of the AIB, the AIB itself can be considered as a new client for ING. Venturing in such a complicated country as Afghanistan is also good publicity for ING.

The Institutional and Government Advisory, the department that employs Arno Van Dijken, has been founded to explore new frontiers and new products for ING. Van Dijken goes on:

> We have ING employees at our disposal with valuable knowledge and experience. We put them in to advise institutions and function as interim managers, as we did in Mongolia and as we now do in Afghanistan. An important part of our work has to do with *financial institutions*. ING has many relations with banks that not only want financing but also want advice. That is an extra product of ING for its clients. We advise a bank on how to be a bank. We also get companies together, even if there is no financing involved. As long as Afghanistan does not have a Chamber of Commerce, we will fulfil that task.

Meanwhile ING has been consulted by the Afghan government about setting up a clearinghouse. For that purpose the IT expert of ING has called in the help of Indian IT experts.

It is widely expected that getting Afghanistan's banking system on its feet again will give a significant boost to economic activity. Van Dijken reckons that:

> the involvement of ING will be more trustworthy in the financial world in general than a purely Afghan bank. Afghanistan is a jungle with a complete lack of regulations. The Afghan Central Bank is the only local bank with some kind of performance, but more banks need to flourish in order to speak of a financial structure again. The Afghanistan International Bank will start off in a vacuum.

Disentangling interests

Putting up a bank in a jungle is something we would like to know more about. How does one manage in a country with an administration on an interim basis, a country where the Central Bank is almost empty, where ethnic groups play shadowy roles in the eyes of outsiders, where warlords rule their own regions, where clans are an important factor but do not figure in the reality of Westerners?

The first step is 'getting to know the right people', trying to find out which people have so much power and influence that they can help an investor. Van Dijken explains:

> Opening the new bank in Afghanistan has had a very long history. That is inevitable to avoid wrong decisions, wrong business partners, or a wrong strategy that can cause a lot of trouble. In Afghanistan you never know to whom you are talking. There is no other option than being quite pragmatic and using the right sources of power. In the interim administration Ashraf Ghani, the Finance Minister, was clearly a man of great influence, also in crediting a bank licence. He pointed out to us which members of government had a strong position, like the Minister of Trade, Mustafa Kazemi. The latter really was of great support. In my presence he managed to get the Governor of the Central Bank on the phone, Anwar Ul-Haq Ahady.[4]

Skills are also needed, as Mr Van Dijken articulates, 'to get a picture of all the interests'. Who has a say in what, and why? Initially ING wanted to establish a bank for commercial facilities and for micro-credit schemes, together with the Aga Khan Foundation.[5]

> The negotiations with the Aga Khan Foundation alone were already tougher than all the other aspects. Our interest was to be a bank manager for a couple of years, but the AKF's interest was to rapidly enter the market with micro-credits through a commercial bank.

Finally, the negotiations failed and ING was left to concentrate on one division, commercial banking.

4   In 2004 he would become the Minister of Finance.
5   A private development foundation established in 1967 by the head of the Ishmael Muslims, the Aga Khan. This NGO is mainly active in Asia and East Africa and has branches in 12 countries.

Then there is another tough part: finding out who are reliable business partners. The Afghan founders of the bank had taken the initiative to contact the Asian Development Bank (ADB). Van Dijken goes on:

> For us these investors are interesting because they are Afghans and professionals. That is very important for the success of the bank. They are all past 50 and wish to return to their home country. They have enterprises abroad and have large reconstruction projects running in Afghanistan. So they are already involved in legal businesses. We have not screened them ourselves but have relied on information from the ADB. I presume that the ADB has closely scrutinised their businesses and their ties with the Afghan authorities. Besides, the Afghan Central Bank should know the background of these investors. Until now we do not have the impression that something is wrong with them.

All in all, ING has explored part of the Afghan jungle with guides such as the ADB and 'the strong men' in the Karzai administration.

Power structures

In the pre-election phase, when ING started up the bank in Kabul, Afghanistan did not have democratic institutions. ING had no other choice than to comply with the existing power structure in the interim administration, or to do nothing. ING chose the first and had to manoeuvre in a culture in which power is considered as a means to create order and in which concentrated power is totally acceptable. Both in social life as in the constitution of the state, strong leaders are highly valued. The head of the clan has absolute power, and in his role of paterfamilias he is entitled to make important decisions. His subjects acknowledge this status and expect him to bear full responsibility for them. Individual freedom is subsidiary to the security of belonging to a group or clan. The men in power use their networks to consolidate or extend their sovereignty. If someone wants to belong to that network, he can count on having to render valued services. This cultural arrangement is not typical just for Afghanistan but is to be found in all Central Asian and Arab countries.

Every high-level Afghan official will try to surround himself with people who are loyal to him, so key positions are preferably reserved for members of the same family or clan. Take, for example, the strong Trade Minister in the interim administration, Kazemi, who had appointed a number of cousins in strategic places. One of them was commercial attaché in Germany; another in Dubai. Two were trade representatives in Iran; one was Chief of Customs in Kabul, and yet another was Head of the Food Supply Office. The Afghan Minister of Defence, Mohammad Qasim Fahim,[6] was also an expert in networking. His cousin was defence attaché in Germany. The three highest posts in his ministry were allotted to members of his political movement (Shur-yi Nezar), consisting of parties who had previously fought against the Soviet occupation. One of them is also the brother of Foreign Secretary Abdullah Abdullah. Almost all Afghan ambassadors were confidants of members of the Karzai administration. Those in the Czech Republic and Egypt were uncles of President Hamid Karzai; those in Bulgaria and Ukraine were cousins of the Minister of Education, Yunos Qanuni.[7] And the ambassador in Kyrgyzstan? He was the brother of the notorious warlord in the North of Afghanistan, Abdul Rashid Dostum.[8]

In Afghan culture the power elite is entitled to privileges. In September 2003 an incident occurred that aroused international indignation but was fully in line with Afghan culture. One day the inhabitants of a poor quarter in Kabul were surprised by bulldozers, protected by some 100 policemen. Even before all 250 inhabitants managed to pick up their belongings, their houses were demolished. Some women and children were wounded during the swift operation. The plot of land happened to be officially owned by the Ministry of Defence and was located close to the district of all the foreign offices. Bad luck for the families, most of them former employees of the Ministry of Defence, who had lived there for 25 years or more, but this was a very suitable piece of land to build residences for ministers and high-ranking officials. The UN rapporteur on housing rights, Miloon Kothari, was in a fury. Property disputes, he warned, can plunge Afghanistan back into conflict. Kothari said the alleged

6   This former warlord has not been reappointed in the administration after the 2004 elections.
7   He challenged Karzai at the elections, lost and did not return in the new cabinet.
8   'Nepotism, Cronyism Widespread in Afghanistan', *Afghanistan Report* 16 (15 May 2003), www.rferl.org/afghan-report.

land-grabbers had taken advantage of Afghanistan's chaotic post-conflict situation to seize property. Kothari stated:

> It is my firm belief that at a time when Afghanistan is in the process of rebuilding after decades of conflict, the governmental authorities should not be involved in any processes that lead to further dispossession of the vast majority of the people of Afghanistan who are already in vulnerable situations.

In an interview he raged that the housing shortage obviously did not count for 'the rich, the people with the right connections, the war lords and the drugs bosses'.[9]

President Karzai immediately promised a full investigation of the matter. But that is a politically very sensitive step, since the Minister of Defence, a Tajik and former commander of the Northern Alliance that helped oust the Taliban, is one of the most powerful men in the government.

The Minister of Education, Yunos Qanuni, and the Governor of the Central Bank, Anwar Ul-Haq Ahady (yes, he too was a candidate for a plot of land) announced at a press conference that their actions had been legal, as the land was owned by the Ministry of Defence. 'I believe in human rights; I support human rights. This is political terrorism,' was Ahady's response to the accusations of the UN. A clear demonstration of two parties whose cultural orientations clash and who both think that they are fully in the right.

'Clean' business partners

Although Arno Van Dijken, the 'architect' of the AIB, did succeed in contacting the right networks to get things done—a prerequisite for any businessman, Afghan or foreign—he still feels that 'in Afghanistan you never know whom you are talking to'. That does not come as a surprise. Apart from the cultural differences, there are specific complicating factors in a country that has been at war for such a long time and where people have had to rely completely on the informal economy. The Karzai administration, eager to encourage invest-

9 Statement of Special Rapporteur on adequate housing, 6 September 2003.

ments, simplified the registration of traders and investors by demand-ing only a credible bank account. That worked, in the sense that by the beginning of 2003 over 1,600 licences had been granted. But Umer Daudzai, who worked in his home country for UNDP and would later become chief of staff to President Karzai, warned: 'To find the so-called clean Afghan business partner is not an easy task. There are allegations that many of the Afghan traders may have made their fortunes through involvement in drug trafficking and smuggling.'[10] Estimates by UNDP and the World Bank are that in the year 2000 alone the contraband trade through Afghanistan amounted to $2 billion, the same amount as was involved in the trade in drugs com-ing from this country.

How clean are ING's business partners in the AIB? Even if it were possible to trace the origin of their wealth, it would still be hard to judge how 'clean' their money is, since they have been doing business in surroundings where, let's say, 'different ethics' were common. If we take the example of one of the shareholders, Farid Maqsudi, it is not to point out that he was wrong or right but to illustrate what is meant by 'different ethics'. Farid Maqsudi is an American citizen, a member of an Afghan family that had built up a commercial empire in the neighbouring country of Uzbekistan. But there he got into big trouble when his brother decided to separate from his wife in 2001. She, Gulnora Karimova, happened to be the daughter of the Uzbek president. This alliance, having been so favourable for the enterprise of the Maqsudi family, turned sour and so did the enterprise. Roz Trading, importing products from Western companies such as Gil-lette, Wrigley, Nestlé, Procter & Gamble and Coca-Cola, was now fair game. The Uzbek authorities liquidated the firm, expelled the family, accused their firm of illegal activities and demanded $12 mil-lion in outstanding taxes.[11] What is more, Uzbekistan asked the American Ministry of Justice to charge Roz Trading for money laundering, tax evasion and bribery. Whatever the truth of the accusations may be, one thing is for sure: they would not have come up if the marriage with the president's daughter had been main-tained.

10   Lecture, 'Possible Private Sector Contributions to the Reconstruction of Afghanistan', at the conference 'Public Bads: Economic Dimension of Conflict', Bonn, November 2002.
11   *Financial Times*, 20 August 2003.

Farid Maqsudi is now CEO of the Afghanistan Reconstruction Company (ARC), an American-Afghan company with large projects such as the construction of the road between Kabul and Kandahar and the construction of a new Hyatt hotel in Kabul (200 rooms, a business centre and luxurious apartments for semi-permanent residents). On the ARC board we find one of the other shareholders of the new AIB, Ishaq Nadiri. He is economics professor at New York University and senior economic adviser to President Karzai. Other principal executives in the ARC are Vice-President Glenn Simpson, formerly working for Roz Trading in Uzbekistan, and Zaher Yakubie, owner of a trading company in, again, Uzbekistan. The ARC, having headquarters in New York and in Kabul, is an important player in the reconstruction of Afghanistan, at least as long as the Americans have such a big say in the country.

The risks

A bank such as ING, lending its name and management to an Afghan 'adopted daughter', takes high risks in a country where corporate behaviour does not run on quite the same lines as the Western idea of ethical entrepreneurship. ING has gained its position in Afghanistan by using the existing power structures through the networks of the present power elite. There is a chance of losing this position as soon as a new elite replaces the old. The new men in power will not feel resolutely obliged towards the business partners of 'the old regime'. New cousins will enter the scene.

A second risk is found in the Afghan shareholders of the new bank. ING trusted the screening performed by the ADB, but their Central Asian way of doing business cannot count on worldwide acceptance. ING has built in some safety valves. Van Dijken fills in:

> The shareholders are put at arm's length of the board. They have no say in decisions about credits or loans, for instance. Of course, one should find out where a big investor gets his money from, but you cannot always completely check everyone's background. That is why our managers always have to report back to our headquarters in Amsterdam, whenever large transactions are involved. Suppose our Afghan stakeholders come up with certain plans, then our management will always put them to the

test of our business principles. We also work closely together with the Asian Development Bank and the International Finance Corporation.[12] They monitor our plans
according to internationally accepted norms and values.

A third risk is possible damage to corporate image. Although Van
Dijken states that ING 'will establish a banking system based on
Western standards', it is easily conceivable that Western stakeholders will see ethical problems in the way the bank operates in the
local market. Especially in a country where the drug trade and smuggling bring in billions of dollars, it is quite impossible to keep 'dirty'
money away. Van Dijken says, 'There is a certain risk of reputation,
since our name is attached to a bank that gets a lot of attention. If the
bank does not function well, it is just plain logic that ING will be held
accountable.' On the other hand Van Dijken is of the opinion that in
a country such as Afghanistan, with such a backlog in development,
'it is impossible to strictly apply the Western view on corporate
responsibility'. In saying this, the task-oriented entrepreneur Van
Dijken shows that he knows how to cope with the role orientation of
the Afghans, as long as it supports the task.

Reconciling the dilemma

For the stability of a war-torn country, a rapid recuperation of the
private sector is vital. Afghanistan cannot count on a perpetual
stream of money from donors, who are already distracted by the
reconstruction of Iraq and will soon also turn to Sudan or any other
country in peril. Although the majority of the entrepreneurs are
reluctant to enter Afghanistan due to lack of security, stable government and efficient infrastructure, investors are slowly trickling in.
That is hopeful, because too much hesitance on the part of investors
diminishes the peace dividend and increases the chance of destabil-
isation. But for the then Afghan Finance Minister Ashraf Ghani[13] this
trickle is too little: about $100 million of foreign investment so far,
mainly in telecommunications and hotels. Ghani called on the

---

12   A member of the World Bank Group, promoting sustainable private-
      sector investment in developing countries.
13   Interview in the *Financial Times*, 13 August 2004.

international private sector to boost legitimate enterprise and prevent the opium industry from swallowing the renascent legal economy, stating that 'If 50 *Fortune* 500 companies invested $10 million each, it would have an enormous impact.' He reckons Afghanistan needs $15 billion in private-sector investment to create a modern state 'that is a cultural and commercial hub'.

Moreover, bustling economic activity in Afghanistan is of great importance for the whole region. Central Asia is a powder keg (Rashid 2002). The neighbouring countries of Turkmenistan, Tajikistan, Uzbekistan, Kyrgyzstan and Kazakhstan all have authoritarian regimes, which are more occupied with their own continuance than with the needs and aspirations of their subjects. Islamic extremism takes by storm millions of unemployed young people. There is also plenty of potential conflict simmering among the Central Asian countries, with disputes over boundaries, access to water, the exploration of gas and oil, the drug trade, etc. If the economy of these nations can flourish, there will be less urge to grab for weapons (International Crisis Group 2003b, 2003c).

Foreign investments are not only necessary to help revive the local private sector, they can also convince Afghan entrepreneurs in the diaspora community to return to their home country—a fact that will help broaden interest in keeping the peace (World Bank 2003a).

Of course it is highly respectable for companies to refrain from investing in Afghanistan as long as there is no escape from complying with the local power games. That can be conceived as ethically justifiable. But it is also unproductive. They neither use the possibility of boosting the private sector nor can they play an 'educative' role.

The situation in Afghanistan requires a way of operating that respects the local culture and at the same time has an ethical justification. ING is venturing down this path. The bank combines pragmatism (getting the strong man in government on the phone) with an ethical aim (developing a trustworthy financial structure in which reliable transactions are viable). The Karzai administration manoeuvres in much the same way. In complicated political situations it reacts with a large dose of pragmatism: depending on the circumstances, the amount of ministers fluctuates between 28 and 34. This is easily ridiculed from the Western point of view, but these moves have the higher motive of preventing the country from falling apart. It is this same motivation that prompts Karzai not to give short shrift to the warlords who maintain their own armies, who provide luxurious palaces for themselves and who will, beyond question, station their own people along the new highway between Kabul and Kandahar to collect an illegal toll. In Afghanistan's current stage of development, there is only one way to deal with them: giving them a role as a legitimate participant in society, so they will start promoting their interests in a peaceful manner (Sedra 2002). Of course, this will not bring their illegal sovereignty to an end soon. Such can only be the outcome of a long process of transition.

Meanwhile, it is essential for ING to take safety measures. The bank risks having to clear out in case of a (undemocratic) change in power. And the bank will surely encounter nepotism and pressure to finance projects for the privileged. In addition, ING is vulnerable to scandal in Western public opinion for not adopting the correct ethical attitude. Part of these safety measures lie in the management of the new bank. Having an important shareholder such as the ADB makes it possible to keep tight control on assignments in the bank and the type of projects eligible for loans and credits. Also, like many other international banks, ING has joined the so-called 'Equator Principles'. These are social and ecological directives of the International Finance Corporation for project financing in emerging markets. Banks that endorse these directives should not put money in businesses that are socially or ecologically detrimental. That means no money for projects that involve forced land expropriation, child labour, or environmental damage. There are also instruments for companies, such as the 'Conflict Risk and Impact Assessment' of International Alert,[14] that can help to provide a picture of the impact they have on conflicts and safety. A growing number of companies in conflict regions also engage an independent institution or consultancy to monitor their activities in order to make timely adjustments in processes and products.

The new bank will have to put much effort into gaining 'a licence to operate'. That comprises relationships with a wide range of stakeholders in the country to find out what the mutual needs and problems are. This is a precondition for trust. It is important to invest in these relations right from the start rather than waiting until after trouble has started. Vital for creating trust is that the new bank is transparent about its activities, especially about the criteria for loans

---

14 An independent, non-governmental organisation that works to generate conditions to end war.

and credits and about the code for handling illegal practices such as fraud, corruption and money laundering.

Of course, in a country such as Afghanistan, it is not easy to find out who the stakeholders are, but that is precisely a reason to make thorough investigations to that end. According to the information on its own website,[15] ING wants to contribute to the socioeconomic development of the communities in which it does business. ING also states that it is committed to 'conduct more of the stakeholder dialogue at a local level in the coming years and to involve local management in that dialogue'. We presume that these ING principles also apply to the new bank in Afghanistan, even if ING contributes only the management. MNCs in Afghanistan encounter the same attitude as those in Iraq: a lot of distrust, both local and abroad, regarding the interests of MNCs in post-conflict countries with an interim administration. Thus it is of the utmost importance to be open about intentions and accountable for the application.

ING could find inspiration in an initiative of the Business Humanitarian Forum (BHF),[16] an international, non-profit organisation which brings business support to humanitarian work and facilitates private-sector investment in post-conflict and developing regions. The BHF, also active in Afghanistan, has selected sectors with good prospects that fulfil the people's needs, such as medicines, food, electricity, construction and communications, projects that fit the 'Afghan National Development Framework'. BHF helps to build partnerships between companies, aid organisations and local authorities and co-operates with the UNDP's Bureau for Crisis Prevention and Recovery. The initiative is interesting because it combines entrepreneurship with knowledge of the local culture and the involvement of the authorities. It is thus the perfect way for the corporate world to get a licence to operate. Co-operation with officially acknowledged organisations would considerably diminish the vulnerability of the image of the new 'Afghanistan International Bank in association with ING'.

Realistically, though, explaining to the Western audience of stakeholders and critical watchdogs how a company in Afghanistan combines pragmatism with ethical business will remain a tough job. The Northern European culture is based on consensus and equality and has no tolerance for a power elite with privileges as is endemic in

15   www.ing.com, with a link to 'ING in society 2002'.
16   Founded in 1999 in Geneva, Switzerland.

Afghan culture. ING will have to be prepared with a well-developed policy prior to possible problems arising. If this is done only after arguments flare up, it will be very hard to come up with convincing arguments.

6
Carrots and sticks

Dilemma: Economic sanctions are a frequently used instrument to bring bad regimes into line. If multinational corporations circumvent an economic boycott, they act unethically, as the bad regime will benefit. But the consequences of complying with a boycott also tend to be unethical, as this hits the weaker in society more than the political elite.

There are moral and political reasons to stick to economic sanctions against Fidel Castro. When the Cuban economy weakened due to the cancellation of the Soviet subsidies, Castro was forced, very much against his will, to allow private enterprise. But as soon as the situation improved, the government abolished every trace of economic freedom. In my opinion the United States should uphold the embargo until Castro's successors introduce political freedom. If the embargo would be lifted now, unilaterally, there is no incentive for change after the Castro era.

The Cuban writer and journalist Carlos Alberto Montaner, in exile in Madrid since 1970, is seen as a differentiated thinker—neither a hard-core Castro-hater nor a fan of the Revolution. But if we ask his opinion on economic sanctions against Cuba, he turns out to be relentless. They are not to be lifted, even if they have failed to undermine the position of El Lider Màximo during the past 40 years: 'Cuba is comparable with North Korea; the dictatorship does not wither in the face of sanctions, nor of aid.'[1] Nevertheless, Montaner is convinced that:

---

1 Quotes from Carlos Alberto Montaner are from an interview with the authors, October 2003.

the worse the economy gets, the more freedom the Cubans will be allowed. Thanks to the economic crisis, the army was reduced by half. Thanks to the crisis the regime allowed farmers to sell their products on the market, and thanks to the crisis relatives from abroad could send money. Castro was obliged to permit private enterprise. But now that his headache is over, the government returns to orthodox Stalinism, including jailing and executing opponents. Therefore, there is only one conclusion: the life of the Cubans gets better if the life of the government worsens, and vice versa.

To underline his standpoint, Montaner sent us a column he wrote for the *Miami Herald* in October 2003. In this piece he turns against former Soviet President Michael Gorbachev, nowadays a celebrity speaker travelling from conference to conference, who went to Miami, the city with the highest density of anti-Castro hardliners, to plead for the lifting the sanctions against Cuba. According to Gorbachev, sanctions are a relic from the Cold War. Of course, Gorbachev's appeal fell flat because right at that time the already poisoned Cuban–American atmosphere was enriched with the new slogan, 'Cuba, terrorist state', following wild accusations of Castro preparing biological and chemical weapons of mass destruction. Talking about Cuba easily puts people out of temper, and so does talk of sanctions.

An ethical aim

Economic sanctions are the most frequently applied penalty for 'disobedient' countries. China, Iran, Zimbabwe, Indonesia, Colombia, India, Pakistan—all these countries are or have been subject to sanctions. Sanctions derive from the idea that it is immoral not to act when leaders starve their people, prepare for war, have their opponents executed, or abuse human rights in any other way. When diplomacy is too feeble, and military intervention too strenuous, sanctions are applied. Sometimes mild and slow—a ban on bank loans. Sometimes hard and sudden—a complete trade and financial blockade.

Economic sanctions have an ethical aim in view. They are meant to combat the evil of failing leadership and prevent the even greater evil of war. But the application of economic sanctions raises a good number of ethical complications.

Just have a look at the countries that promulgate economic sanctions. These are almost always countries with strong economies, and, without exception, they impose sanctions against countries with weak economies.[2] Sanctions, though, are not imposed on every country with a disagreeable government, but only if the punishers' own economic or political interests are at stake. The US is far in the lead in meting out penalties; it did so 110 times in the last century.[3] In the majority of the cases this was a unilateral act, sometimes with the lone support of Great Britain. From the 1990s on, more sanctions derived from the United Nations Security Council[4] (see Table 6.1), instigated by the US. Whenever the Security Council dealt with proposals to lift or ease sanctions, obstruction came from the US and Great Britain, thus creating the image that not the UN but the Anglo Saxon alliance is the global policeman. This image is reinforced by the impression that the US and Great Britain are selective in choosing their targets, merely acting upon offences that hurt their specific interests. Thus Iraq was hit with sanctions after its invasion of Kuwait, whereas countries such as Israel, Morocco, Turkey and Indonesia have got away with occupying (parts of) neighbouring territories.

The principal idea behind economic sanctions seems to be founded on a universal ethical attitude, but the interpretations and applications are not in the least universal. Poor countries cannot issue them; they can only suffer from them. If the wrongdoer is a befriended nation, nothing happens. If the wrongdoer has to become an ally, like Pakistan in the 'war against terrorism', sanctions are speedily withdrawn.

Add to that the fact that the efficacy of economic sanctions is unclear. Instead of leading to a regime change, they bring great humanitarian suffering. According to the American Institute for International Economics,[5] sanctions only bring about the desired change in one out of three cases. Other researchers come up with

---

2 Research by Gary Clyde Hufbauer on 116 cases of sanctions showed that the average economy of the punishing countries was 187 times larger than the economy of the punished country.

3 *Washington Post,* 12 July 1998.

4 Before 1990 only twice: Southern Rhodesia (1966) and South Africa (1977). After 1990 12 times: Iraq, former Yugoslavia, Libya, Somalia, Liberia, Haiti, Angola, Rwanda, Sudan, Sierra Leone, Afghanistan, Ethiopia and Eritrea.

5 Gary Clyde Hufbauer, Jeffrey Schott, Institute for International Economics, 1998.

Year of issue	Country	Motivation	Sanction	Key changes
1990	Iraq	Invasion of Kuwait	Full trade embargo	Oil-for-food programme in 1997; all sanctions lifted in 2003
1991	Yugoslavia	Civil war	Arms embargo	Economic sanctions on Serbia and Montenegro (1992); trade embargo Bosnian Serbs (1994); sanctions lifted 1995
1992	Liberia	Civil war	Exports and arms embargo; asset freeze; travel restrictions	Ban on rough diamonds (2001)
1992	Libya	Failure to turn over PanAm suspects	Arms embargo; asset freeze; travel restrictions	Lifted in 2003
1993	Angola	Civil war	Oil and arms embargo; asset freeze; travel restrictions	Air and travel ban (1997); ban on UNITA diamond exports (1998)
1993	Haiti	Failure to return to democracy	Oil and arms embargo; asset freeze	Lifted in 1994
1994	Rwanda	Civil violence	Arms embargo; aid suspension	Ban on arms sales lifted in 1995
1996	Sudan	Failure to hand over suspect of assassination of Egyptian President Mubarak	Travel restrictions	

TABLE 6.1 UN economic sanctions issued since 1990 (continued opposite)

Year of issue	Country	Motivation	Sanction	Key changes
1997	Sierra Leone	Civil war	Trade and arms embargo; travel restrictions; ban on rough diamonds	Ban on oil lifted in 1998
1998	Somalia	Civil war	Arms embargo; aid suspension	
1998	FR Yugoslavia	Kosovo	Arms embargo	Lifted in 2001
1999	Afghanistan (Taliban)	Failure to turn over Usama bin Laden	Asset freeze; flight ban; freeze of funds owned by Taliban; arms ban	
2000	Ethiopia/ Eritrea	War	Arms embargo	Lifted in 2001
2004	DR Congo	Civil war	Arms embargo for all armed groups and militias in North and South Kivu and Ituri	
2004	Ivory Coast	Civil war	Arms embargo; travel restrictions, assets freeze	

TABLE 6.1 (from previous page)

more gloomy results and even question the prime example of successful sanctions—those against the apartheid regime in South Africa. Like Usha C.V. Haley, Associate Professor of Business at the University of Tennessee, who concluded after studying 322 MNCs that divested from South Africa in the 1980s that the fall of apartheid could not be ascribed to an economic boycott that was widely evaded (Haley 2001).

But even if there was a causal relation between the end of apartheid and the international boycott, it still is an irreproducible success. It only works in countries with a white minority regime and an economy that is completely intertwined with that of the 'punishers'. Such countries no longer exist.

Smart sanctions

Dramatic humanitarian side-effects complicate the ethical justification of economic sanctions. A 1999 study concluded that post-Cold War sanctions may have contributed to more deaths than all 'weapons of mass destruction' used throughout history (Mueller and Mueller 1999). The most recent example is Iraq, subjected to a barrage of sanctions for over a decade, including a comprehensive trade blockade. The economy collapsed after 1990, and an estimated one million people, mainly children, died due to the effects of the sanctions. Every Iraqi, except for the regime and its supporters, felt the blow.

Nevertheless the population did not turn against Saddam Hussein, mainly because in their view the West measured by two standards: it intervened in Iraq but not in Israel. Saddam even received sympathy from many Arab countries, since it was their arch-enemy wielding the stick. This illustrates what the Norwegian professor of peace studies, Johan Galtung (1967), wrote: sanctions often achieve the opposite aim; the population ranges itself on the side of the victimised leader, and nationalistic feelings are roused. Thus in Iraq economic sanctions failed to remove the evil of failing leadership and failed to prevent the even greater evil of war.

Then there is the damage of economic sanctions brought upon third countries. Sanctions against Iraq were harmful to the economies of 21 other countries, since trade with Iraq became unlawful. The trade embargo against former Yugoslavia meant a huge rise in transportation costs for other countries, forced to divert from their normal travel routes. Ironically, even the most fervent upholder of sanctions, the US, was hit: in 1995 alone, the US lost between $15 billion and $19 billion in export income due to its own sanctions against 26 countries.[6]

The humanitarian disaster resulting from the sanctions against Iraq was one of the reasons why in the mid-1990s the idea of 'smart' sanctions grew popular. An abundance of policy studies followed, scrutinising all varieties of sanctions: suspension of aid, air and travel restrictions, arms embargoes, comprehensive trade restrictions, bans on cultural exchange, inhibition of foreign investment, denials of most-favoured-nation status, bans on multilateral lending,

6   Gary Clyde Hufbauer, Jeffrey Schott, Institute for International Economics, 1998.

etc. The studies revealed what was already widely known: sanctions are a blunt instrument;[7] they are seldom successful and mainly hit the most vulnerable people. Within the UN a laborious process was set up to replace the present regime of sanctions by targeted measures with more impact and less collateral damage.[8] But a growing range of independent scientists is rejecting the whole idea of economic sanctions. Joy Gordon, American philosophy professor at Fairfield University (Connecticut) and author of numerous articles on sanctions, is completely against the idea of modifying economic sanctions. The aim of economic sanctions, she states, is no other than strangling the economy in order to make the leaders change their minds. That inevitably leads to hurting the civilian population. That is why Gordon proposes the completely opposite idea. The present supposition is that sanctions are a legitimate instrument in foreign politics and in international law, unless they lead to too many innocent victims. The supposition, however, should be that sanctions are illegitimate and inhuman and should not be applied in foreign policy or to enforce international law, except for those specific situations in which they are proven not to hurt the innocent (Gordon 1999).

Action-oriented cultures

Why do Western countries so frequently apply economic sanctions if they lack success and add to human suffering? The explanation can be found in the urge 'to do something', something less violent than war but more forceful than carpeting the ambassador. This attitude is characteristic of action-oriented cultures such as the American or the British. In action-oriented cultures people want to proceed to a concrete, clear and imaginative action. If that move is not quite

7   On 3 January 1995 the Secretary-General of the UN called sanctions 'a blunt instrument'. In a supplement to his Agenda for Peace he wrote: 'They raise the ethical question of whether suffering inflicted on vulnerable groups in the target country is a legitimate means of exerting pressure on political leaders whose behaviour is unlikely to be affected by the plight of their subjects.'
8   On 17 April 2000, the Security Council established the Working Group on General Issues on Sanctions to study ways to improve the effectiveness of UN sanctions. Four years later, the proposed outcome document remains under active consideration.

successful, modifications can be discussed, such as alleviating measures for the local population. But what cannot be discussed is the principle that action is necessary. Jagdish Bhagwati, the influential Indian economist and professor at Columbia University in New York, once said in an interview:[9]

> You can't blame US policymakers for thinking that, somehow, trade sanctions are the way to spread goodness around the world. In a way, that is a cultural notion; Americans seem to adopt the Superman model very quickly.

Decisiveness is highly valued in action-oriented cultures and should not be hampered by a long process of learning lessons from the past. The fact that the Castro regime survived 40 years of sanctions is not reckoned with in the decision to impose yet another sanction. In 1998 American President Bill Clinton commiserated that the US had become 'sanctions happy'.[10] Shortly before, however, he had authorised sanctions against India, Pakistan, Cuba, Iran and Libya.

Although NGOs generally do not have an action-oriented organisational culture, they do apply marketing strategies with such a cultural preference. They are genuinely worried about humanitarian disasters caused by ruthless tyrants, so they cry for action against a Mobutu, a Milosevic or a Mugabe. Supporters of activist NGOs want to see a message that is easy to communicate. It is very common for the NGO world to lobby governments to impose sanctions. Long-term solutions that deserve accurate analysis or balanced consideration are less attractive.

In action-oriented cultures, differences in applying sanctions do occur. Canada, for instance, has a more moderate view than the US. In the case of Burma, Canada is of the opinion that MNCs are responsible for their own decisions to invest, but the government puts pressure on these MNCs to implement a code of conduct. The EU, with a foreign policy that is heavily influenced by the French–German axis, is inclined to search for dialogue with a contested regime. That is why the EU does not join the US in boycotting Cuba, even after the US turned on European businesses dealing with Castro.

---

9 *Harvard International Review*, Fall 2000.
10 Reuters, Bill Clinton in interview with CBS News, 20 June 1998.

Process-oriented cultures

There is little room for 'the carrot' in action-oriented cultures. Partly accommodating demands equals not accommodating at all, to the extent that, as is illustrated by the run-up to the latest Gulf War, if not all conditions are met, punishment is the only right answer. As action-oriented cultures are dominant in sanctions policies, African and Asian ways of conflict resolution do not stand a chance. These process-oriented cultures prefer a gradual and less visible approach, which gives Westerners the impression that nothing is happening at all. Take the example of Zimbabwe. African political leaders are, of course, troubled by the course of their Zimbabwean 'brother', Robert Mugabe. They do not idly watch him destroying the economy of his country, but they try to influence him. They do this not by excluding or isolating him but by drawing him and his supporters into their meetings and by offering rewards such as honour and status. This approach, however, is obstructed by Western countries that keep insisting Mugabe should be treated as a pariah by African leaders.

Process-oriented cultures prefer rewards as an instrument. The Liberian President Charles Taylor refused to step down, although he was on the list of 'most wanted' at the International Court of Justice of Sierra Leone because of his role in the civil war in that country. Only when the Nigerian government offered him a comfortable hiding place in exile did he give in. This meant that the war plotter Taylor could escape conviction for his crimes, but it also meant that he was rendered harmless and that the peace process in Liberia accelerated. However, the US administration rejected this solution and in November 2003 brought a proposal to Congress to withdraw $75 million of aid to Nigeria if the country would not extradite Taylor to the International Court of Justice.

Another example of a process-oriented approach is to be found in Burma. The military junta did not manage to win the battle against the warlords from different ethnic groups. The junta then decided to call for a ceasefire and to persuade the warlords to sign agreements that benefit them. The never-ending guerrilla wars now belong to the past. The Karzai administration in Afghanistan (see Chapter 5) undertakes similar efforts by trying to include warlords in the system. From a Western point of view there is much to be said about this approach, but the fact is that tens of thousands of civilians are no longer being squeezed between warring parties.

People in process-oriented cultures are more apt to reckon with all complexities. They prefer step-by-step solutions that respect all parties, however brutal or obnoxious. Experiences from the past are not ignored but are seen as precious lessons. That is exactly why Fidel Castro was warmly welcomed in 1998 in South Africa by President Nelson Mandela. Cuba had played an important role in the liberation wars in Southern Africa in the 1980s. In one of his speeches Mandela said to Castro:

> Because your support has also come through teachers, builders and doctors whom you sent to our continent and through the training of many South Africans in your schools and universities, we are still reaping the harvest as we rebuild our country.[11]

The man who, as ANC leader, called for sanctions against the apartheid regime, now declared himself an adversary of the American trade embargo against Cuba, saying:

> As the beneficiary of international solidarity that helped make it a member of the community of free nations, democratic South Africa is proud to be among the majority of nations who affirm the right of the Cuban people to determine their own destiny, and that sanctions which seek to punish them for having decided to do so are anathema to the international order to which we aspire.

'Economic terrorism'

A typical representative of a process-oriented culture is the prominent Burmese writer, artist and former political prisoner, Ma Thanegi. She considers economic sanctions 'no different from economic terrorism, because they deteriorate the suffering of the poor'.[12] Ma Thanegi is no longer active in politics, but far from retiring she continues to publish furious articles on political topics in the *Far Eastern Economic Review*, among others. Advocates of eco-

---

11   Nelson Mandela, speech in Paarl, 4 September 1998.
12   Quotes from Ma Thanegi are from an interview with the authors, February 2003.

nomic sanctions are not in her good graces. 'What is more important: change for the benefit of the population, or satisfying emotions?' she recently wrote sarcastically. 'My argument against sanctions is that they hurt the people more than the government, and that there are other ways to bring about change other than the idealistic and futile strategies of sanctions, boycotts and isolation.'

When we met in Rangoon, Ma Thanegi explained why she calls these strategies futile:

> The position of the military regime is as firm as it was 13 years ago, when the boycotts started. The low-income un-skilled people—most of whom do need jobs to feed their families on a daily basis and keep a roof over their heads— are the ones most hard hit. They are the ones without savings or the skills needed for high salaries. The wealthy owners of factories may lose money through boycotts, but is this fair exchange, when tens of thousands of people— especially young girls—lose their jobs? The military do not mind, because these are not their daughters that work in a factory.

If sanctions are not successful, what then are other means to move the regime in the direction of democratisation? Ma Thanegi replies:

> Economic development and political change can go to-gether. We have to get out of our isolation; we have to modernise; we need employment. I would encourage re-sponsible Western companies to start investing here. If Western investors would start relations with high-level people in government, they can broach matters concern-ing democratisation. That would be positive. Asian busi-nessmen do have these relations, but they will not talk politics. And, please, let tourists come. Every single visi-tor brings in new perspectives, which is so important for a country that has been cut off from the rest of the world for such a long time. Unfortunately, the belief in the cor-rectness of economic sanctions has taken root so deeply that it has become incorrect to call for pragmatism. It has become politically incorrect to openly criticise the course of the opposition party NLD or its leaders. If you do, you are instantly accused of treason. A call for realism imme-diately leads to the judgement 'pro-junta'.

Pressure on multinationals

Multinationals investing in countries subjected to sanctions will sooner or later have to think over their position. The bigger the leverage for sanctions, the stronger the pressure on MNCs to abide by them. The pressure, naturally, does not come from the government of the host country, since it benefits from foreign companies. It comes from the government of the home country, which has a whole range of instruments to discourage evasion of sanctions. And of course the pressure comes from activists and consumers' organisations, who are a powerful force.

The reasoning that not complying with a boycott is unethical forces companies to choose between two evils. If they abide by the sanctions, they lose money through divesting and harm the most vulnerable people in society. If they do not abide by the sanctions, they are considered unethical, causing damage to their reputation that in the long run is also financially detrimental.

Divesting is not only a burden to the company, it also remains to be seen whether the aim of sanctions comes any closer. The most probable scenario is that other companies fill the gap left by the Western MNCs. The result is that the economy of the country is not hurt, but the employees and the local population are hurt. Peter Frankental, manager of the Amnesty International Business Group, was at the time not in favour of the international call on Premier Oil to retreat from Burma (Blyth 2003):

> We don't take a view of whether or not companies should operate in a particular area. We argue that they should consider human rights and they should be aware that they cannot be neutral players, but there are two reasons why we would not call on Premier Oil to withdraw from Burma. For one thing we are not allowed to go there, so cannot truly assess its impact. More importantly, we believe that governments should pressurise each other and that the regime in Burma will only change when there is sufficient political and diplomatic pressure to do so. It is easier to focus on companies than on governments, but ultimately it is less effective.

Former Africa CEO of Heineken, Jean-Louis Homé, absolutely never wanted to submit to pressure to boycott a country, as was the case after the *coup-d'état* in Burundi. Homé explains:

We stay because of our people, and because the presence of a foreign company is fundamental. You can set an example if you behave properly, you transfer knowledge, exchange people from Europe to Africa and vice versa. In 1996 I called Ahmedou Ould Abdallah, former UN special envoy in Burundi, about the pressure on Heineken to leave Burundi. He urged us to stay, stating that Burundi's government would try to keep the brewery going anyhow and wouldn't hesitate to use forced labour. And if the brewery would nevertheless close down, it would harm the economy in such a way that ethnic conflicts would be worsened, he said. I am convinced that decent companies are part of the development of a country.[13]

Reconciling the dilemma

What then are the alternatives for a responsible company in countries that are subjected to boycotts or sanctions? Given the fact that the universal principle behind sanctions can have a variety of local interpretations, an entrepreneur will have to decide according to the situation. There is no standard recipe. Several circumstances will have to be taken into consideration. For instance, is the targeted country a signatory to international agreements on human rights, labour conditions and environmental protection? Can the company bring about a change for the good? Will the company have a chance to live up to its own ideals of corporate citizenship? If the answers are negative, the company is in danger of adding to the misery of a country and its inhabitants. But if one of the answers is positive, it is not by definition unethical to invest in such a country.

Situations in failing states are complex by nature. But if companies are able to assess the risk of investments in the most complicated countries, then they are very well able to also comprehend the risk of ethical entrepreneurship. That requires a good analysis of who the stakeholders in that specific country are. These are not only shareholders, subcontractors, employees and customers but also local and national governments, the inhabitants, and local and international

13 Quotes from Jean-Louis Homé are from an interview with the authors, December 2002.

NGOs. In discussion with these stakeholders, one can expect to come up with a sustainable strategy. The strategy should be built along the line of applying at least one criterion: can the company bring about a change for the good? If the company believes so, it has to be open to criticism from its stakeholders and be willing to accommodate assessments of its projects by a neutral party.

In case an MNC has already invested in a country hit by economic sanctions, it is relevant to ask the question: which causes more damage, leaving or staying?—taking into account damage to the company itself and also damage to the local population. If a company decides to leave, it should be responsible for an exit strategy that reduces the negative impact as much as possible.

A big challenge for companies will be to foster public understanding of its decision to ignore economic sanctions. Since sanctions have the image of striving for a just cause, they are always applauded by idealistic people. The applause is less loud if those economic sanctions comprise an individual act by a single country and hence have less leverage. But if these sanctions have extensive support and target a tyrant, guilty of brutal abuse of human rights, public opinion turns rapidly against a company 'dealing with villains', notwithstanding its degree of corporate responsibility. This is something companies will always have to reckon with. In such a case it is useless to challenge the justification of sanctions. Ideals and convictions are hard to contest. Yet ideals can weaken if they are confronted with other ideals, such as the ideal that companies can contribute to stability by *not* complying with sanctions, thus dragging a country out of the prelude to war.

7
Profits and ideals

Dilemma: To meet the challenges of conflict regions, multi-national corporations and non-governmental organisations need to team up. The not-for-profit and profit sectors, however, are looking at each other with deeply rooted distrust. The MNC goes for profits, the NGO for ideals. Neither of them can compromise.

Colombia—a country rich in resources but plagued by internal conflicts. Guerrilla, military, police and right-wing militia finance their operations through the drug trade, abduction and blackmail. At least 1.5 million civilians have been displaced by violence. The drug mafia has puppets in all vital sectors of society: the judiciary, trade, army and government. One of the poorest and most violent regions in the country is Magdalena Medio. The central government is almost absent and the local government is 'infected' by warring factions. Over two-thirds of the inhabitants live below the poverty line in an atmosphere of distrust, fear and polarisation.

Around 1995 the Diocese of Barrancabermeja contacted the state oil company Ecopetrol to co-ordinate efforts to reduce violence and poverty. It was the start of an ambitious plan to be carried forward by the population itself, the Magdalena Medio Regional Development Project.[1] The Colombian central government sustained the project with $5 million (a loan from the World Bank) and Ecopetrol added $1.25 million. In 1998 the project was launched, co-ordinated by the NGO Consortium for Development and Peace Magdalena Medio (CDPMM). The project fitted with the strategy of the government to support regional and local activities aimed at targeting the

---

1 More information at www.worldbank.org/conflict.

causes of violence and at the same time achieving social development. In the case of Magdalena Medio, the role of the Catholic
church was vital, since it was the only body that could count on at
least some authority among the population. By 2004 the project had
proven to be so successful that both the EU and the World Bank now
contribute financially.

Venezuela—another country rich in resources and plagued by
political and social unrest. Half the population tries to survive in the
informal sector. In a period of ten years the percentage of people
living in extreme poverty doubled from 11.8 to 23.5.[2] The inequity
between rich and poor is poignant. The political turbulence and
failing governance scare away foreign investors. Gold resources in
the state of Bolivar are rich, but gold mining by large companies has
a troubled past and present. Conflicts between the mining companies, the local population, small independent gold miners and the
government are abundant. In the early 1990s, a consortium consisting of the Canadian mining company Placer Dome and the Venezuelan state company Corporación Venezolana de Guayana (CVG)
acquired a mining concession in Las Cristinas. When they were
instantly confronted with tough social problems, they developed a
plan to tackle the high unemployment and the lack of schools and
hospitals in the region. But the extractive operations were delayed
over and over again and, when around 1999 the gold price dropped,
Placer Dome decided to pull out of the consortium. Its place was
taken by another Canadian firm, Crystallex, which adopted the
existing development plans. To implement the necessary measures,
the mining consortium created a partnership with the organisation
Business Partners for Development,[3] the Venezuelan Ministry of
Health, the governor of the state of Bolivar, the World Bank and local
NGOs. The results are impressive. A health centre has been set up for
12,000 inhabitants, medical workers are trained and facilities for safe
potable water have been provided. Solutions have been found for the
local groups of independent goldminers, who feared unemployment. And the tripartite partnership has grown into a forum for
dealing with all the other social problems in the region.

2   Source: World Bank. The criterion for extreme poverty is earning less
than $1 per day.
3   Business Partners for Development was a three-year project, now ended,
that   researched   tripartite   partnerships;   www.bpd-
naturalresources.org.

Partnerships

These kinds of partnerships between MNCs, governments and NGOs spring up like mushrooms. It is noticeable that the extractive industry is conspicuous in taking part in these coalitions. In a way this is not surprising, since this branch specifically has ample experience with misery in its areas of operations, causing so much financial loss that the companies are compelled to embark on a different course. The misery is partly caused by the industry's operations. Extractive industries have a notorious history of ignoring property rights of landowners, displacing local populations and neglecting environmental spin-off. But beyond their control is the 'endemic' misery, caused by war, internal strife, failing governance or criminal gangs. If these extractive companies want to survive, they will have to look for other ways of managing the ecological and social impact of their presence in the region and for ways of solving or preventing conflicts. They are now seriously seeking a different course, but since they lack expertise in these fields they have started engaging professionals.

Consultancy for conflict-sensitive companies has in itself become an important 'industry'. Take for example Amnesty International.[4] The British section of this human rights organisation has even founded a specialised branch, the Business Group, which has 25 consultants at its disposal to advise companies on their performance in high-risk regions. Peter Frankental, manager of the Business Group, says, 'It is an irreversible trend that companies consider respect for human rights as part of their core business. They are standing in line to contact us.'[5] This does not mean, however, that Amnesty International partners with companies. Frankental states, 'We remain neutral, impartial, and do not accept payments from companies. Our role is warning and advocacy.' Right from the start, Amnesty International has involved itself with the predictable impact of the oil pipeline from the Caspian Sea to the Mediterranean. This pipeline, constructed by a BP-led consortium, runs through Azerbaijan, Georgia and Turkey. The first two countries suffer from economic crisis and inter-ethnic strife; Turkey has a poor human rights

4   Amnesty International developed human rights guidelines for companies. See www.amnesty. org.uk/business/pubs.
5   Quotes from Peter Frankental are from an interview with the authors, October 2003.

reputation. Hence, NGOs are worried about the economic, social and ecological consequences of the pipeline. Amnesty International, not wanting to choose between either investing against a high social price or not investing at all, has strongly advocated a third option: incorporating basic rights of the population in the design of the investments. Amnesty International continually tests whether the arrangements between the energy consortium and the governments of the three countries still comply with international regulations on human rights. Frankental says, 'After we issued a critical report on the pipeline [Amnesty International 2003b], all parties concerned—BP and its partners, the World Bank and all the credit banks—got in touch with us.'

But it is not only the extractive industry looking for partners to stabilise the situation in conflict regions. Among the MNCs that have joined Business Partners for Development are representatives of all sectors: IT companies (Microsoft), water companies (Aguas de Barcelona) as well as manufacturers of sports shoes (Nike). Parties that for a long time past have been adversaries—MNCs, NGOs and governments—are more often than not obliged to put aside their differences. Companies simply lack the expertise to work on 'sustainable development' and are watched with distrust by the beneficiaries. They need NGOs that have thorough knowledge of the local circumstances, are experts in community building and can count on ample social acceptance. From their part, NGOs have an interest in co-operating with companies, since these are important players, especially when the government is not inclined to invest in basic social services. Companies can put in capital, machinery, transportation and organisational skills, and they sometimes have easy access to high-level government officials. Another reason NGOs have an interest in entering into partnerships is that they can motivate companies to operate responsibly. Governments, the third party in the coalition, understand that they have a lot to gain from the combined funding and professionalism, provided this does not weaken their authority.

As a matter of fact, these tripartite partnerships potentially offer a perfect escape from the many pitfalls in conflict regions. *Potentially*, because in practice parties often feel that they have to abandon part of their core business if they start co-operating. Many among them cannot imagine a possible reconciliation of the dilemma in which neither the profits nor the ideals are compromised. One of the reasons is mutual distrust.

Distrust

The distrust is especially bitter between two of the three partners—the MNCs and the NGOs. For many of the NGOs, to co-operate with MNCs is like being in league with the enemy. Their spirit is well reflected in the works of two heroines of the anti-globalisation movement, the British economist Noreena Hertz (Hertz 2002) and her Canadian equivalent Naomi Klein (Klein 2001). According to Hertz, MNCs are so powerful that they 'destroy the fabric of democratic societies', and Klein warns that large companies do not sell physical but emotional products, changing and perverting the cultural landscape. The ideological row between the corporate world and the NGO world naturally contains a lot of rhetoric, such as the popular assertion that the capital represented by MNCs is much larger than the gross domestic product (GDP) of many countries. Studies showing that this comes down to 'comparing apples to oranges', indicating that MNCs are surprisingly small compared to the GDP of many nation-states and that there is little evidence for the increase of the economic and political power of MNCs in the last few decades, have no impact on this emotional debate (de Grauwe 2002).

Rhetoric is also amply used by companies. The American Enterprise Institute, an influential, conservative think-tank, gave a striking example of caricaturing in June 2003. At the launch of its new website,[6] the institute warned of the power of NGOs who, by the way, since 1996 have been running websites[7] to do exactly the opposite, exposing the power of corporations. The American Enterprise Institute criticises the trend of companies to support NGOs. Its website was inaugurated with a conference entitled 'The Growing Power of an Unelected Few', dominated by speakers who pictured NGOs as an unaccountable power and an increasing threat to capitalism and to the foreign policy of the American administration. The organisation stated:

> Politicians and corporate leaders are often forced to respond to the NGO media machine, and the resources of taxpayers and shareholders are used in support of ends they did not intend to sanction. The extraordinary growth of advocacy NGOs in liberal democracies has the potential

6 www.ngowatch.org
7 For instance the American www.corpwatch.org and the British www.corporatewatch.org.uk.

to undermine the sovereignty of constitutional democra-
cies, as well as the effectiveness of credible NGOs.

With such a controversy, it is hard to imagine a rapid reconciliation
between the two sectors.

Organisational culture

Partnerships are complicated not only by distrust but also by differences in organisational culture. MNCs and NGOs have developed
strategies and organisational structures according to their differing
goals: profits and ideals. In the way they operate, we recognise the
cultural orientations of task and role.[8] An MNC, taking profitability as
a criterion for all decisions and judgements, values personal responsibility and measuring results. The goals of an NGO are not measured
in terms of loss or profit; the results are qualitative. For NGOs the
criterion is whether the way the budget is spent will meet the expectations of the sponsors and public opinion.

As a watchdog, NGOs have a positive role in society. However, they
will not be effective if they demand that companies give up their core
business, making a profit. A company can be attacked for the way it
makes a profit but not for wanting to make a profit. This can be
illustrated by the case of Greenpeace, demanding that ExxonMobil[9]
reduce its production of fuel because it harms the ozone layer. That
goal will not be reached, but nevertheless this Greenpeace action
was successful in the sense that all newspapers published pictures of
activists in tiger costumes occupying the offices of ExxonMobil. The
message had reached the public and the sponsors.

An NGO needs to survive, just like a company. They have people on
their payroll and need cash. Careers are planned and pursued. This
is a fact of life in the corporate world but less obvious in the case of
the not-for-profit world. A strategy is built to add value, be it money
or ideals. A prerequisite for this is that the organisation stays alive.
No actions may go against this condition, and some actions are
targeting only this condition. Survival must take priority over added
value.

8   See Chapter 2.
9   *The Economist*, 7 August 2003.

These differences (see Fig. 7.1), deriving from the difference in survival techniques, goal setting and organisational culture, are exactly the reason why NGOs and MNCs have problems in opening up to each other's arguments.

Mutual accusations

Luc Zandvliet can hardly ever be found in his office in Cambridge, Massachusetts, as he is constantly travelling. To Nepal, with its civil war and its disputes on the construction of dams. To Sri Lanka, where tourism and industry are cautiously reviving since a fragile peace agreement has been signed. To Nigeria, where oil drilling in the Niger Delta has caused a lot of trouble, or to neighbouring Cameroon with its problems in the logging industry. In Papua New Guinea he studied how the proposed closing of a gold mine could proceed without leading to conflicts with the local population. In Burma he is engaged in the dialogue between NGOs and energy companies. He consistently looks for the negative or positive impact of the daily operations of MNCs on conflicts.

This former employee of Médecins sans Frontières (Doctors without Borders) is now head of the Corporate Engagement Project,[10] which develops practical management tools for stable and productive relations in the societies in which corporations work. According to Zandvliet, 'Companies in conflict regions will always have to deal with NGOs either because NGOs claim to be the mouthpiece of the local population or because NGOs give international exposure to the activities of companies.'[11]

He is convinced of the fact that MNCs and NGOs in conflict regions need each other and can benefit from each other. But the largest obstacle to co-operation is 'an absolute lack of trust', which leads to mutual accusations. Zandvliet goes on:

> Companies say that NGOs use them as proxy targets to
> further their own agendas, such as the anti-globalisation

10 A project of the American consultancy Collaborative Development Action.
11 Quotes from Luc Zandvliet are from an interview with the authors, September 2003.

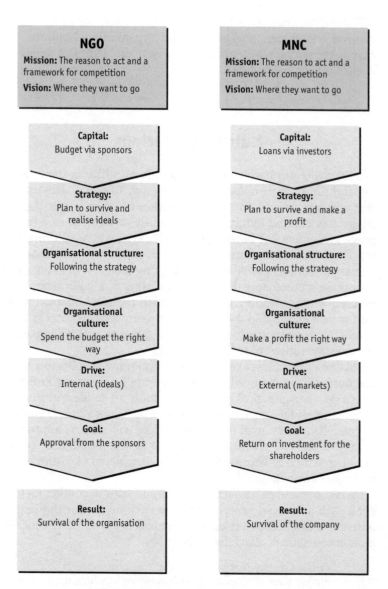

FIGURE 7.1 Not-for-profit and profit organisations: differences and similarities

agenda. They say that NGOs are not accountable to anybody whereas companies are held accountable by their
shareholders, their customers and other stakeholders.
They picture NGOs as powerful institutions that are more
trusted by society and the media, making it impossible for
companies to win a debate. And they say that it is impossible to change the opinion of NGOs, since they feel they
are morally right. NGOs mirror these critical views when
speaking of companies. In their eyes companies, however
socially responsible they pretend to be, only further their
own agenda of increasing profits. They are not accountable to anybody, just as the World Trade Organisation or
the International Chamber of Commerce are non-elected
bodies that only further the corporate agenda. Companies are powerful, have the means to influence politics
and hire the best lawyers to defend their interests. And
you cannot change the behaviour of companies because
they are arrogant and stubborn. The consequence of
these reciprocal views is that companies and NGOs hardly
ever talk to each other, so they never really get to know
each other.

Luc Zandvliet makes a distinction between 'activist NGOs' and 'service NGOs'. Co-operating with the latter category, comprising aid
organisations such as Save the Children or Care International, is not
much of a problem.

They stick to their mandate, even if they receive money
from companies to execute their work. Much more complicated is the co-operation with NGOs whose main activity is lobbying in the field of human rights, democratisation, rights of indigenous peoples or environment. Their
aim is raising awareness and influencing public opinion,
which is quite a different kind of mandate. If both activist
NGOs and companies strive for a similar goal, ameliora-
tion of the living conditions of the people, companies still
tend to see them as a threat.

A turn of the tide

However, there is a turn of the tide, now that companies are more
compelled to ethical entrepreneurship and NGOs are becoming more

in favour of market-based solutions for development. Especially in countries with a weak or failing government, NGOs are more apt to choose the corporate world as a partner in their striving for better conditions for development.

In June 2003 an important study was published that predicted a seismic shift: rising numbers of NGOs engaging with business to bring about positive societal change (UN Global Compact 2003, with SustainAbility[12] and UNEP). This prediction resulted from interviews with over 200 NGOs, businesses, foundations and other opinion formers, dealing with the identification of the challenges these organisations will face in the 21st century. 'The good news for NGOs is that they are emerging as vital ingredients in the health and vitality of markets,' said John Elkington, chair of SustainAbility and one of the report's authors.

> They are also highly trusted, far more so than business or governments. The bad news is that unless they recognise and address growing financial, competitive and accountability pressures, their impact will be significantly reduced. For those that respond intelligently and in time, the prize is to be amongst the most influential institutions of the 21st century.

The relationship between NGOs and the private sector will change significantly, according to the interviewees. Of course, NGOs will continue campaigning companies, but this method is only effective in clear-cut cases of companies with famous brands (Coca-Cola, Shell, Esso). A more effective strategy is to put pressure on individual companies through their customers, subcontractors, shareholders and boards to change their business model. One step further are partnerships with the private sector to bring about social development. The report concludes that the importance of these partnerships will increase.

Oxfam International, a confederation of 12 development organisations working in over 100 countries, regards business as an essential part of economic growth and development and tries to maximise the positive and minimise the negative impact of the private sector in developing countries. Its campaigns at the macro level against global trade rules that are detrimental for producers in third-world countries are well known. The Oxfam-affiliated organisations undertake

12   www.sustainability.com.

a large variety of engagements with businesses. Jeremy Hobbs, executive director of Oxfam International,[13] states:

> Some engagement is critical and derives from complaints of local NGOs who are unhappy with business conduct. But, for instance, the engagement of Oxfam Australia with the mining company BHP Billiton has over time grown from hostile to very constructive.

BHP Billiton has created a forum on Corporate Responsibility as one mechanism to address contemporary challenges. The forum is a regular dialogue between BHP Billiton senior management and a range of NGOs, which provides an opportunity for both parties to debate topics ranging from local mine site issues to global issues such as climate change. The Australian branch of Oxfam has initiated the Business Ethics Forum, to encourage dialogue between the private sector and the community. Constructive engagement also appeared possible with the consumer goods company Unilever. Jeremy Hobbs explains:

> The management of Unilever wants to do business in a pro-poor manner. Unilever has asked the British and Dutch branches of Oxfam to investigate whether their local investments in Indonesia lead to poverty reduction. There are real possibilities to engage with *bona fide* companies.

The director of the Dutch branch of Oxfam, Jan Bouke Wijbrandi, is in favour of engaging the private sector in poverty alleviation, but he stresses the importance of engaging the government as a third partner:[14]

> The government should as a minimum develop rules for corporate social responsibility, for transparency, for reporting, and for the performance of subcontractors. In conflict regions the law is by definition weak. It is very hard to make companies comply with non-existent rules, as it is very hard to monitor how companies behave in these territories. In my opinion, partnerships between NGOs and MNCs are viable in such situations, but you will have to make very strict arrangements.

13 Quotes from Jeremy Hobbs are from an interview with the authors, July 2004.
14 Quote from Jan Bouke Wijbrandi is from an interview with the authors, October 2003.

Reconciling the dilemma

The reconciliation of the dilemma 'profits versus ideals', the apparent conflicting goals of MNCs and NGOs, starts with the identification of their common goals. NGOs in conflict regions strive for peace and stability, democratisation, respect for human rights, increasing prosperity, more equity in income and protection of the environment. Companies in conflict regions want to achieve a safe working environment for their employees, continuity of productivity, extension of their market share and a positive image among all their stakeholders. These interests and goals overlap to some extent, and that is where co-operation can be concentrated and developed. But at the same time partners will have to respect each other's core business. An MNC will only step into a partnership if it can abide by its core business and does not have to get involved in activities that endanger its profitability. The same goes for an NGO: it is all right to collaborate with the private sector in designing plans for the development of a region, but not at the cost of its own priorities.

Business Partners for Development (BPD) (2002) has put quite some effort into finding out what it entails to give partnerships more content and has distilled some suggestions for their survival. First, a company should have a clear picture of what it wants to achieve through a partnership in order to find the right combination of partners that have the same goals in mind and have a mandate to act. Equally important for success is that the partners have common goals that do not jeopardise the core business of each individual partner. BPD also recommends considering contacts with less obvious partners, especially organisations that have no financial interests. They can be valuable partners as they can bring in original ideas, have a sound distance and may be highly esteemed. The mining company Freeport-McRoRan, heavily criticised for calling in the Indonesian security forces at their operations in the Indonesian province of Papua, contracted Gabrielle Kirk McDonald as special adviser on human rights. Ms Kirk McDonald is a famous human rights lawyer, who has also been a judge at the International Criminal Tribunal for the former Yugoslavia. Freeport McRoRan also contacted Amnesty International and the Robert F. Kennedy Center on Human Rights to develop its new human rights policy. And in the area of its operations, the mining company created a channel to communicate with the local population.

Confidence building

All co-operation is founded on two basic principles. First comes the willingness ('yes, I want to co-operate'), soon to be followed by confidence ('. . . and I trust you'). Building confidence is not a matter of a contract with penalty stipulations, because in that case a party will only be loyal as long as that is more profitable than breaking the contract. Confidence is only built through getting to know each other, by looking for facts instead of emotions, by reciprocal understanding, by being predictable in actions and by being transparent. It is not necessary to develop a common organisational culture. Parties only need to support each other's goals and understand that to contribute to the other's core business is adding value to its own core business.

Researcher Luc Zandvliet states:

> It is vital that people talk to each other. If not, they will always stick to their own opinion. I am aware of the fact that it is difficult for companies and NGOs to take the first step for a dialogue. But exchanging views is not the same as giving in. NGOs often feel instantly compromised, and MNCs have this macho attitude of 'who has the right to say that we are wrong?' NGOs sometimes are very self-righteous and have a culture that forestalls taking the first step. Confrontations hinder discussions; why not start with agreeing on the facts? Take the case of Burma: why not start finding out how much of the assumption of forced labour or land mines is correct? After that you can decide on what these facts mean. Companies want to know on whose behalf NGOs speak and what their real aims are. They feel that NGOs misuse them for their own hidden agenda, that they spread false news and deliberately never correct it. It makes company executives furious and I cannot blame them because, if NGOs distribute false information, they also undermine the credibility of the people with real complaints. But companies are also strong in spreading false information. The ensuing mutual lack of trust leads to exaggeration and polarisation, which undermines the basis for a common case.

To build confidence between MNCs and NGOs, both parties will have to abide by codes of conduct. Oxfam International's executive director Jeremy Hobbs expands:

> We try to balance between our right to maintain a critical
> voice and the need to act in good confidence. We act to a
> high level of ethics. If we co-operate with a company, we
> sign a Memorandum of Understanding, in which we
> clearly state in which case we cannot maintain confiden-
> tiality.

But codes of conduct are not sufficient. Both parties will have to be
transparent about their practices. According to Luc Zandvliet,

> In countries like Burma or Indonesia there is no such
> thing as a 'just solution'. So companies will have to make
> public how they deal internally with matters that have no
> simple solutions. It is sometimes amazing to read the offi-
> cial propaganda of some MNCs, whereas at the same time
> their country managers can tell you straightforwardly
> how complicated it is to do business in the countries con-
> cerned. Companies would do better if they would be open
> about their struggle to remain in Burma and about their
> internal considerations. There is no instant solution for
> operating in countries like Iran, Libya or Burma. If you
> pretend there are, you lose your credibility.

A good way of building confidence is creating a formal structure
for dialogue between MNCs and NGOs on concrete matters as well as
ethics. It is best to do this before scandals, calamities or quarrels have
arisen. An example is the arrangement between the Norwegian oil
company Statoil and Amnesty International to train all managers
sent to non-European countries in human rights and dealing with
conflict situations. Statoil operates in countries such as Azerbaijan,
Angola, Nigeria, Venezuela and Brazil. Managers are taught how to
deal with bribery, corruption and other difficult matters. Amnesty is
a reliable partner for Statoil, stated Geir Westgaard, Statoil vice-
president for country analysis and social responsibility. 'We are
increasingly confronted with conflicts and problems that are new to
us. Amnesty can systematically help prepare our people for these
situations.'[15]

Luc Zandvliet would recommend that every company arrange for
structural contacts with activist NGOs in order to prevent a relationship that is solely defined by problems. He points to Shell as an
example of best practice. Since 1995 the oil company has held meetings three or four times a year with NGOs such as Amnesty Inter-

national. The NGOs are very satisfied with this dialogue, which gives them the opportunity to discuss Shell's policy on human rights. Much to the reassurance of the NGOs, Shell does not send its PR manager to these meetings but flies in the manager who is responsible for the topics discussed. When the NGOs demanded that Shell stop delivering fuel to the Sudanese air force, which was systematically bombing civilian targets, Shell decided to comply but asked for some time to dissolve all contracts.

Zandvliet would welcome a wide application of this example of Shell:

> A company merits a lot of credit through personal meetings with people who are directly responsible for decisions. This creates a confidential relationship with open communication channels between the NGO and the company's headquarters, which results in parties not resorting to alarming the public if something is happening. Also, another nice side-effect is that NGOs hold each other accountable whenever one of them violates the rules of the game.

Accountability

A hot issue in the relationship between MNCs and NGOs is accountability. Both parties blame each other for the lack of it. For a partnership it is indispensable to come up with measurable goals and to make all partners accountable for the results. Luc Zandvliet again:

> Sometimes I ask NGOs what they think a company should do to gain confidence. They often answer that a company should stop its operations. NGOs are very good in analysing the failures of a company, but they fall short in indicating solutions. Preferably MNCs and NGOs should study what is attainable for the company and acceptable for the NGO. At least there should be a final goal. Companies would like to know what they should do to deserve a positive assessment, what makes them acceptable in the eyes of NGOs. In my view, NGOs should specify more steps than merely pointing out what is wrong.

An NGO should also make clear who it effectively represents. Zand-vliet goes on:

> International NGOs have another perspective than local NGOs and they, in their turn, have other perspectives than the local population. I saw this happen in Papua New Guinea, where a mining company dumped waste directly in the river. International NGOs yelled in alarm, 'This is not allowed, not in Europe, not in the US, so neither in Papua New Guinea; close down that mine.' The local NGO, sponsored by international NGOs, however, did not favour the idea of closing down the mine, since that would mean the end of all kinds of advantages, such as the schools, clinics, bridges and roads. But the local NGO was squeezed between the demands of the sponsoring NGO and its own wish to talk about other solutions than the exit of the company. That is why we started discussions with people living along that river. They told us their dogs and pigs had died from the polluted water, but that they could live with that if they were compensated. This is a strong example of 'who is talking on behalf of whom?'

On the other hand, companies should be very clear about their intentions. As Peter Frankental of Amnesty's Business Group comments,

> We are not against dialogue with companies, but what we condemn is their using this dialogue as window dressing, printing prominently on their websites that they have relationships with Amnesty. That kind of stuff is misleading and cannot be a base for genuine co-operation.

But he does not believe in putting this as a kind of condition for co-operation with companies: 'Preliminary conditions do not create safety; they can not prevent the possibility of things going wrong.'

Zandvliet signals hesitation among companies to open up for NGOs, but he strongly encourages them to follow this line:

> If companies in conflict regions do not have NGOs on their side, they will never be completely successful. companies should not strive to be loved but to be respected. In their turn, NGOs should not ask companies to change a bad regime but just ask them to do their utmost to behave well in situations where no simple solutions are available.

8
Scenarios and story telling

> Exotic birds skim the water, past fishermen paddling lazily
> to their bow-nets. A boat full of monks is on its way to the
> pagoda. Evening comes with a choir of crickets and fires lit
> on the hillsides.

**Inle Lake in Central Burma is a heavenly spot. Hotel manager Sein Thun
is not aware of any boycott on tourism to Burma. On the contrary, after
the bomb attack in Bali, tourists have shied away from Islamic countries, and Buddhist Burma is enjoying increasing popularity. The standard of living of the people around the lake has gradually risen, notices
Sein Thun: 'In the past, people could hardly afford a bamboo house on
the water; now they build brick houses on the shore.'[1]**

**But with prosperity comes pollution of the lake, and another of his
worries is the easy money young people make in tourism: 'It turns them
lazy.'**

Sein Thun is a soft-hearted and friendly man, always receiving his
guests with a personal welcome and acting like a father to his employees. 'We are all Buddhists; we bring loving kindness to people,
houses and all living creatures,' he explains. This lecture on Buddhism appears to be a gentle prelude to expressing his great fear that
Burma will be contaminated with sex tourism, just like neighbouring
Thailand. He dreams of a flourishing tourism industry, but without
pollution and moral disfigurement. He has a point. His daily ritual of
receiving new groups of Italian, German and French tourists with
traditional music brings in a lot of money. Not only the Chinese
investors benefit, also the dozens of employees, their families, the

---

1   Quotes from Sein Thun are from an interview with the authors, February 2003.

suppliers of rice, cabbage and fresh fish, and the laundry women in the villages. But there are drawbacks. Tourism imports new wants and new values, and it might soon fill the lake with jet skis and turn the laundry women into pole dancers.

Tourism—the advantages can change into disadvantages in a wink. In the 1990s the US administration eased travelling restrictions to Cuba, hoping the Cubans would be inspired by positive American values, supposedly a strong weapon against communism. The latter failed, but the development of a taste for male and female prostitution was quite successful.

Cambodia is another country that faces the disadvantages of tourism. This industry is of great importance for the reconstruction of the war-torn country, since there is money to be made with only minor investments. Cambodia has a prime tourist attraction with Angkor Wat, the 800-year-old temple complex that is so impressive that many people think of it as one of the seven wonders of the world. Meanwhile, Thailand earns a lot more money from Angkor Wat than Cambodia because most tourists fly in from Bangkok for a day. And there are harmful side-effects, such as the theft of hundreds of statues from the temples and escalating tensions between the Cambodians and Thai immigrants.

For Thailand, tourism has been of great importance for economic development. But Burmese hotel manager Sein Thun sees Thailand as an ogre because that country is happy to accommodate tourists with an appetite for very young virgins.

Tourism is ambivalent. It has the potential for socioeconomic development and cultural achievement, but at the same time it can have a disruptive influence on local communities and the environment.

A scenario

Tourism is the largest industry in the world, and it has a strong impact on economic growth and employment.[2] With its side-effects on food production, construction, transportation, telecommunica-

2 According to the World Travel and Tourism Council, tourism generates over 10% of total global GDP and accounts for 200 million jobs, direct and indirect.

tions and production of consumer goods, broad segments of society can benefit from this industry. It is even imputed to be a branch that fosters peace, since people from different cultures get to know and appreciate each other.[3] Would it be possible to exploit tourism in conflict regions in such a way that it is compatible with the goals of peace and stabilisation, preventing the negative impacts on society? In other words, could Sein Thun's Utopia become reality?

Let us take Inle Lake as a virtual case. Suppose a plan were made to develop tourism in such a way that it improves the lives of everyone. The Inle Lake becomes a lasting, attractive destination for many tourists. The local population is able to choose from a large variety of jobs, so that dependence on fishing decreases and the beautiful lake maintains its ecological balance. The Internet, newspapers and English classes connect the formerly isolated inhabitants with the rest of the world. In the long run this creates a self-assured middle class with the ability to become a countervailing power towards the government. In the slipstream of tourism, new companies will become interested in investing, diversifying the economy, which will finally enable the impoverished country to bring its standard of living up to that of its neighbours, Thailand, China and India. These new companies lobby the government to arrange for essential facilities such as a modern and reliable financial infrastructure with tax laws that foster a balanced development of the country. Talented young people no longer have to take refuge in foreign countries, since universities reopen their doors and vocational training is abundant. And the rebels in the jungle find out that there is a more attractive prospect than the never-ending stumbling in the mud with a rifle on their shoulder.

What conditions could make this Utopia viable?

3   See the website of the International Institute for Peace through Tourism, www.iipt.org. IIPT leader Louis d'Amore says, 'Every traveller is potentially an ambassador for peace.' IIPT is working on a '21st Century Agenda for Peace through Tourism'. See also the British NGO Tourism Concern, promoting ethical entrepreneurship, www.tourismconcern.org.uk.

Regulation

Whenever the tourism sector sees new options in new locations, there are competitors in the field. No doubt among them are investors and tour operators who are interested only in the money and have no ethical concern whatsoever. It is very unlikely that the Burmese government will have the policy, the capacity or possibly even the will to make regulations for investments in the tourism industry. So it will be imperative to design an internationally accepted code of conduct for the complete chain in tourism, from the tour operator to the hotel owner. Among the thousands of existing codes of conduct,[4] there is, strangely enough, not one specifically for companies in conflict regions, although it would be beneficial to all parties.[5] Such a code protects both the local population and highly rated companies against less accountable entrepreneurs. A code of conduct for the tourism industry in conflict regions or in countries with failing governance should contain requirements on safety, human rights, environmental protection, labour standards, intellectual property rights, corruption, transparency, etc.[6]

To successfully develop a tourism industry that acts at a high ethical level, co-operation of the government is indispensable. This, now, is quite an extraordinary operation in a country such as Burma, with a government that is so easily irritated by external interference and so allergic to ethically inclined issues. The military junta deeply dislikes foreign influence and tries to ban any foreigner who might touch on the subject of human rights or democratisation. Ample freedom of movement, on the other hand, is granted to Chinese, Thai

---

4   Europe alone has 27,000 codes of conduct for companies, sometimes for an individual company, sometimes for a whole sector. There is also a variety of international guidelines for enterprises, e.g. UN, International Chamber of Commerce, Organisation for Economic Co-operation and Development.

5   Those available include 'Voluntary Principles on Security and Human Rights', signed by the British and American administrations and a large number of companies in the extractive industry including Texaco, Chevron, BP, Conoco, Freeport McRoRan, Rio Tinto and Royal Dutch/Shell. Renowned international NGOs, such as Amnesty International, Human Rights Watch and Business for Social Responsibility, support these guidelines.

6   In developing guidelines for companies in conflict regions, it is important to consider their usefulness for other cultures and traditions.

or Singaporeans who indulge in illegal transactions (such as smuggling, logging or establishing monopolies), which are in no way beneficial to the 'common' Burmese.

However, there is a chance of finding an opening for dialogue with the Burmese government. The junta is desperately in need of money and is internally divided over the present unimpeded possibilities for Asian companies to rob the country of its resources. Finding a sustainable income by developing tourism in an internationally accepted fashion might persuade the junta to enter negotiations that offer a welcome perspective. It would be worth trying.

Intermediary

But doing business with such a 'bad' regime is very risky. Even if the tourism industry comes out of these negotiations with the best guarantees and arrangements for ethical operations, companies can still be accused of sustaining that bad regime. One way to minimise this risk is by handing over the negotiations with the government to an impartial, well-respected institution. Such an intermediary could be an international NGO or possibly even a 'consortium', consisting of respected lawyers, scientists and diplomats with an unthreatening reputation in the eyes of the junta. With some creativity and imagination, a successful consortium could be installed. Consider the possibility of inviting high-level Japanese and Australians to play a prominent role. They have relatively easy access to members of the junta and are not by definition distrusted by any party involved. Creativity is also needed to make the right arrangements between the intermediary, the government and the tourism industry. At stake is not merely a joint investment in roads, telecommunications, construction and transportation; there are important goals to be realised, such as protecting nature, respecting local cultures, preventing environmental harm, abolishing forced labour, conserving historical monuments, fighting corruption, etc. In other words, the three parties involved would have to agree on a large number of issues, and they would have to trust each other on the implementation of the agreements.

Although much political intuition and imagination is required, the picture we present is not totally utopian. Some elements of our virtual case have been realised in Egypt, a country that has exploited its vast archaeological wealth as a tourist attraction but combined it with the implementation of strict regulations. Supported by a wide range of internationally renowned scientists, the government has taken measures to protect its cultural heritage, imposing heavy penalties for infringement. By giving the local private sector a fair share in the increased prosperity, the population has an interest in stability. If tourists are threatened by fundamentalist Muslim attacks, the government finds the majority of the population on its side when it turns against Islamic extremists.

Pitfalls

If we now return to the virtual case of the Inle Lake, we can discern many of the ethical dilemmas described in previous chapters. An important pitfall is framed in the co-operation with the Burmese authorities. Just as the ING bank in Afghanistan strategically made use of the existing power structures to find its place in the market, the tourism industry will have to find access to influential members of the Burmese junta. What makes Burma an even more challenging location than Afghanistan is the notorious reputation of Burma in the field of corruption. According to Transparency International,[7] the country ranks high on the corruption scale. Ethical entrepreneurs will have a hard job in avoiding these practices. The intermediary and the tourism industry will have to stand up against corruption and negotiate guarantees that bribes will not be requested, regardless of whether by the most high-ranking general or the most humble customs officer.

A second pitfall can become manifest in the co-operation between the tourism industry and the intermediary that we created in our scenario, the buffer between the government and the corporations. Each has their own agenda and mutual distrust will be lurking around the corner, never far away. Parties will have to invest in finding appropriate means of communicating and decide on the common goals. A precondition is to respect each other's core business.

7   The Transparency International Corruption Perceptions Index 2004 names Burma together with Chad, Nigeria, Bangladesh and Haiti as the five most corrupt countries in the world. See www.transparency.org.

The intermediary institution or consortium will have to accept that the tourism and travel branch will join only if there is profit to be gained; the tourism branch will have to accept that the intermediary will break off the negotiations if there are not enough ideals to be realised.

The third pitfall is the danger of taking over government tasks. This danger is manifold. With tourism companies investing in roads, bridges, healthcare and training, the government may grab the opportunity to spend its budget on other non-development items such as private jets, military tanks or beautiful mansions. And the private sector providing public services can give the population the false impression that this is not the government's responsibility.

In our scenario of involving the tourism sector in a strategy that enhances peace and stability, we want to emphasise the importance of paying respect to the interests of *all* stakeholders. This puts high demands on the quality of the communication. Right from the start *all* stakeholders will have to be informed about the intentions and plans. Failures are inevitable if they are not involved in the decision-making process and if they do not get a feeling of ownership. These stakeholders are not only sponsors and shareholders but all the Burmese parties involved, including local retailers and entrepreneurs of all sizes. Beyond that, there should be intensive communication with the Burmese opposition, which is certainly in favour of enhancing prosperity, but not if that means that the junta will pocket the prestige and use it as justification to prolong its undemocratic practices. Also, international public opinion will be suspicious about investing in enjoyable holidays in a country subjected to boycotts and sanctions due to persistent abuses of human rights.

New tensions

Another realistic danger looming is that the tourism sector, however ethically it operates, will create new tensions. There is a strong link between the 40 years of military rule in Burma and ethnic conflict. In practically all regions of the country, but especially the north and the east, ethnic minorities aspire to independence or autonomy. Temporary ceasefires come from arrangements between government, army and rebel leaders, that cannot always bear the light of day. Travel organisations will not limit their holiday offerings to the idyllic Inle Lake, but would like to organise, say, adventurous eco-trips into the jungle. Maybe the central government would at a certain point even allow this. But foreign companies, not fully aware of the history, traditions and culture of the host country, could unintentionally cause new conflicts. They will have to acquire a thorough knowledge of the standpoints of local parties and their interests. And these interests can vary from unwritten land rights to monopolies on drug trade.

China considers Burma to be its back yard, having a large influence not only on politics but also in trade—from televisions to weapons. In a town such as Mandalay, another fine tourist location, Chinese economic domination is meeting with increasing aversion among the Burmese. Signs abound that this aversion can lead to an outburst of violence, as has happened before in Southeast Asian countries with a wealthy group of ethnic Chinese. The tourism industry will certainly touch on this sensitive issue, because many local hotels are owned by Chinese. It is not likely that these hotel owners will enthusiastically support an 'ethical approach' to tourism if there is no gain in it for them.

Also, there is lingering animosity between the Thai and the Burmese. Like all neighbours, these two countries foster mutual prejudices. The Burmese think of the Thais as smart and materialistic, and the Thais see the Burmese as stupid and lazy (Sim 2001). Currently, Thailand flies in large groups of tourists daily to visit the temples of Bagan, so Thailand has a big interest in tourism. Of course, newcomers to the tourism market will investigate who their competitors are, but in this case they will have to reckon with possible prejudice of the Burmese against the Thais. If they fail in this respect, they could easily create new tensions.

One step further

Executives of MNCs, interviewed in previous chapters, stated that they contributed to peace and stability through their core business. These were companies in the financial sector, extractive industries and producers of consumer goods. In our scenario we looked at the tourism industry as ethical entrepreneurs in a conflict region. Virtual or real, the companies remained within the boundaries of their original mandate, putting a product on the market and going for profit.

Some CEOs interviewed said that they saw no other role for themselves in conflict regions. Even as business diplomats, they want to stick to their frame of reference. A wider responsibility is rejected because of their belief that companies have neither the mandate nor the leverage to become 'peace agents'. That is supposed to be more in the field of intergovernmental or non-governmental organisations. These organisations, however, do not share this view. Although they admit to having the mandate and the public confidence to play the role of peace agent, they know that they lack (economic) power. They adhere to the view that companies should use their presence in a country to put pressure on the warring parties.

Is a reconciliation of both views possible? Yes, we believe it is. Reconciliation lies in combining and maximising the power of both sectors: the public confidence of the non-governmental or intergovernmental organisation, and the economic power of the corporate sector. In our scenario the tourism industry should throw in its lot with the success of the intermediary NGO in negotiations with the government. The intermediary and the corporations present one common front. If they agree on the conditions for and the method of promoting tourism in Burma, leading to economic prosperity *and* stability, the intermediary can represent the corporate sector in negotiating with the government and can make a stronger point because of the economic power behind it. The government will either have to take the proposals of the intermediary seriously or accept that this opportunity for development will evaporate into thin air when the tourism industry retreats.

In this scenario, both the corporate sector and the intermediary NGO benefit from each other's principal features, without compromising their own core business. It may sound paradoxical, an NGO representing an MNC, but in this case it is the ideal reconciliation of the dilemma.

Peace or justice?

What exactly do we strive for in conflict resolution: justice before peace or peace before justice?

Economic sanctions have until now appeared to be a blunt instrument in making malevolent regimes change their ways, as is demonstrated in the cases of Haiti, Panama, Cuba, Sudan, Angola and Burma. Military intervention, another option to end a conflict, is always unattractive, and when deemed inevitable there is still no guarantee of success (Somalia), or a situation is created in which military presence seems to be endless (Bosnia, Kosovo, Afghanistan, Iraq). Sometimes the military force is so limited that there is hardly any impact, as we have seen in Liberia and Congo. And, if the guns have successfully been silenced, this has to be followed by rapid post-war reconstruction, visible to the entire population, or else instability and new conflicts loom.

Meanwhile, conflicts in Aceh, Nepal, the Palestinian Territories and Ivory Coast, to name just a few, are left to diplomats to solve. But diplomacy alone is often unable to cope with the complex reasons behind conflicts.

If there is one lesson to be learned from recent history and the globalising economy, it is that new, unorthodox means of conflict prevention and resolution are wanted and greatly needed. Bringing MNCs into action as business diplomats could be such an unorthodox way.

Utopia? Sure!

Proving it to be unrealistic? Easy!

But unattainable? With such a strong motivation as self-interest?

Bibliography

Amnesty International (1998) *Human Rights Guidelines for Companies, 1998*, www.amnesty.org.

—— (2000) *Sudan: The Human Price of Oil*, www.amnesty.org, May 2000.

—— (2003a) *Business and Human Rights: Towards Legal Accountability*, www.amnesty.org, January 2003.

—— (2003b) *Human Rights on the Line: The Baku-Tblisi-Ceyhan Pipeline Project*, www.amnesty.org, May 2003.

—— (2003c) *Iraq: On Whose Behalf? Human Rights and the Economic Reconstruction Process in Iraq: Recommendations to Governments, Companies and the United Nations*, www.amnesty.org, June 2003.

Anderson, Mary B. (1999) *Do No Harm: How Aid can Support Peace—or War* (Boulder, CO: Lynne Rienner).

Bailes, Alyson J.K., and Isabel Frommelt (eds.) (2004) *Business and Security: Public–Private Sector Relationships in a New Security Environment* (published for SIPRI by Oxford University Press).

Berdal, M., and D.M. Malone (eds.) (2000) *Greed and Grievance: Economic Agendas in Civil Wars* (Boulder, CO: Lynne Rienner).

Blyth, Alex (2003) 'Analysis: Premier Oil and Burma—Who Are the Real Winners?', *Ethical Corporation Magazine*, 18 February 2003.

Bolongaita, Emil, and Vinay K. Bhargava (2003) *Challenging Corruption in Asia: Case Studies and a Framework for Action* (Washington, DC: World Bank).

Brill Olcott, Martha (2002) *Kazakhstan: Unfulfilled Promise* (Washington, DC: Carnegie Endowment for International Peace).

BPD (Business Partners for Development) (2002a) *Endearing Myths, Enduring Truths*, www.grsproadsafety.org → Reports and Publications → Business Partners for Development (World Bank).

—— (2002b) *Putting Partnering to Work*, www.grsproadsafety.org → Reports and Publications → Business Partners for Development (World Bank).

Cameron, Kim S., and Robert E. Quinn (1999) *Diagnosing and Changing Organizational Culture* (Reading, MA: Addison-Wesley).

Carnegie Commission (1997) *Preventing Deadly Conflict: Executive Summary* (Washington, DC: Carnegie Endowment for International Peace).

Collier, Paul (2000) *Economic Causes of Civil Conflict, and their Implications for Policy* (Washington, DC: World Bank).

—— (2003) *Breaking the Conflict Trap: Civil War and Development Policy* (Washington, DC: World Bank and Oxford University Press).

Corporate Engagement Project (2002) *Myanmar/Burma Report, 2002*, www.cdainc.com/cep.

—— (2002–2003) Yadana Gas Transportation Field Visits, November 2002, April/May 2003 and December 2003.

Cousens, Elizabeth M., and Chetan Kumar (2001) *Peacebuilding as Politics: Cultivating Peace in Fragile Societies* (project of the International Peace Academy; Boulder, CO: Lynne Rienner).

Daudzai, Umer (2002) *Possible Private Sector Contributions to the Reconstruction of Afghanistan*, www.inwent.org/ef-texte/publicbads/daudzai.htm.

Davies, Robert (1999) *Corporate Good Practice in Post-Conflict Business 'Opportunities': Six Principles for Partnership Action* (London: IBLF [International Business Leaders Forum]).

De Grauwe, Paul, and Filip Camerman (2002) 'How big are the big multinational companies?', www.econ.kuleuven.ac.be.

Economist (2003) 'American Values: Living with a Superpower', *The Economist*, 2 January 2003, www.economist.com/printedition/PrinterFriendly.cfm?Story_ID=1511812.

Elliott, Charles (1999) *Locating the Energy for Change: An Introduction to Appreciative Inquiry* (Winnipeg: International Institute for Sustainable Development).

Friedman, Thomas L. (2000) *The Lexus and the Olive Tree: Understanding Globalization* (New York: Anchor Books).

Funakawa, Atsushi (1997) *Transcultural Management: A New Approach for Global Organizations* (San Francisco: Jossey-Bass).

Fussler, Claude, Aron Cramer and Sebastian van der Vegt (eds.) (2004) *Raising the Bar: Creating Value with the UN Global Compact* (Sheffield, UK: Greenleaf Publishing).

Galtung, Johan (1967) 'On the Effects of International Economic Sanctions, with Examples from the Case of Rhodesia', *World Politics* 19.3 (April 1967).

Gissinger, Ranveig, Nils Petter Gleditsch and Håvard Hegre (2002) 'Globalization and Internal Conflict', paper for the World Bank project 'Understanding Civil Wars, Crime and Violence through Economic Research', May 2002.

Global Witness (1999) *A Crude Awakening: The Role of the Oil and Banking Industries in Angola's Conflict and the Plunder of State Assets* (London: Global Witness).

Goldwyn, R., and J. Switzer (2003) *Assessments, Communities and Peace: A Critique of Extractive Sector Assessment Tools from a Conflict Sensitive Perspective* (London: International Alert).

Gordon, Joy (1999a) 'Using a Pick-Ax for Brain Surgery: The Ethics of Economic Sanctions and their Predictable Consequences', Kroc Institute Occasional Paper, 15.

—— (1999b) 'A Peaceful, Silent, Deadly Remedy: The Ethics of Economic Sanctions', *Ethics and International Affairs* 13.

Govearts, Didier (ed.) (2000) *Conflict and Ethnicity in Central Africa* (Institute for the Study of Languages and Cultures of Asia and Africa, Tokyo University of Foreign Studies).

Haley, Usha (2001) *Multinational Corporations in Political Environments: Ethics, Values and Strategies* (Hackensack, NJ: World Scientific).

Hertz, Noreena (2002) *The Silent Takeover: Global Capitalism and the Death of Democracy* (New York: The Free Press).

Holliday, Chad, Stephan Schmidheiny and Philip Watts (2002) *Walking the Talk: The Business Case for Sustainable Development* (Sheffield, UK: Greenleaf Publishing).

Hufbauer, Gary Clyde, Jeffrey J. Schott and Kimberly Ann Elliott (1990) *Economic Sanctions Reconsidered* (2 vols.; Washington, DC: Institute for International Economics, rev. edn).

Huijser, Mijnd (2002) *Managing Mindsets: An Appreciative Inquiry into Cultural Differences*, www.cmc-net.org.

International Alert (2000) *The Business of Peace* (International Alert, Council on Economic Priorities and the Prince of Wales Business Leaders Forum; www.international-alert.org).

—— (2003) *Transnational Corporations in Conflict-Prone Zones: Public Policy Responses and a Framework for Action* (authors J. Banfield, V. Haufler and D. Lilly; International Alert; www.international-alert.org).

—— (2004) *Small Arms Control in Central Asia* (authors John Heathershaw, Emil Juraev, Michael von Tangen Page and Lada Zimina; Eurasia Series, 4; International Alert; www.international-alert.org, April 2004).

International Business Leaders Forum (2002a) *The Business of Enterprise: Meeting the Challenge of Economic Development through Business and Community Partnership*, www.iblf.org.

—— (2002b) *Human Rights and Business: A Geography of Risk* (with Amnesty International, www.iblf.org.).

—— (2002c) *Building Partnerships: Co-operation between the United Nations and the Business Community* (with the UN, www.iblf.org).

International Committee of the Red Cross (2000) Forum: *War, Money and Survival*, www.icrc.org.

International Crisis Group (2002a) *Myanmar: The Politics of Humanitarian Aid*, www.crisisweb.org.

—— (2002b) *Central Asia: Water and Conflict*, www.crisisweb.org..

—— (2003a) *Myanmar Backgrounder: Ethnic Minority Politics*, www.crisisweb.org.

—— (2003b) *Central Asia: Last Chance for Change*, www.crisisweb.org, April 2003.

—— (2003c) *Peacebuilding in Afghanistan*, www.crisisweb.org, September 2003.

—— (2004) *Myanmar: Sanctions, Engagement or Another Way Forward?*, www.crisisweb.org, 26 April 2004.

ILO (International Labour Organisation) (1977) *Tripartite Declaration of Principles concerning Multinational Enterprises and Social Policy,* www.ilo. org/public/english/employment/multi/index.htm.

Klare, Michael (2001) *Resource Wars: The New Landscape of Global Conflict* (New York: Metropolitan Books).

Klein, Naomi (2001) *No Logo* (London: Flamingo).

Mack, Andrew (2001) *The Private Sector and Conflict* (Cambridge, MA: Harvard Program on Humanitarian Policy and Conflict Research).

Mahbubani, Kishore (2002) *Can Asians Think? Understanding the Divide between East and West* (Hanover, NH: Steerforth Press).

Mathews, Dylan (2001) *War Prevention Works: Fifty Stories of People Resolving Conflict* (Oxford, UK: Oxford Research Group).

Moody-Stuart, Mark (2001) 'Putting Principles into Practice: The Ethical Challenge to Global Business', speech during the World Congress of the International Society of Business, Economics and Ethics, São Paulo, Brazil, 19 July 2000.

Mueller, John, and Karl Mueller (1999) 'Sanctions of Mass Destruction', *Foreign Affairs,* May/June 1999.

Nelson, Jane (2000) *The Business of Peace: The Private Sector as a Partner in Conflict Prevention and Resolution* (International Alert, the International Business Leaders Forum and Council on Economic Priorities).

—— and Jonas Moberg (2003) 'Rebuilding Bridges, Opportunities and Challenges for Responsible Private Sector Engagement in Iraq's Reconstruction', IBLF Policy paper, 3.

Newton, Andrew, and Malaika Culverwell (2003) *Legitimacy Risks and Peace-Building Opportunities: Scoping the Issues for Businesses in Post-War Iraq* (London: Sustainable Development Programme Royal Institute of International Affairs, August 2003).

OECD (Organisation for Economic Cooperation and Development) (2000) *Guidelines for Multinational Enterprises,* www.oecd.org.

—— (2001) *Public Policy and Voluntary Initiatives: What Roles Have Governments Played?,* www.oecd.org.

—— (2003) *Business Approaches to Combating Corrupt Practices,* www.oecd. org.

—— (2004) *Guidelines on Corporate Governance,* www.oecd.org.

Rashid, Ahmed (2002) *Jihad: The Rise of Militant Islam in Central Asia* (New Haven, CT: Yale University Press).

RFE/RL (Radio Free Europe/Radio Liberty) (2003) 'Nepotism, cronyism widespread in Afghanistan', *Afghanistan Report* 16 (15 May 2003), www. rferl.org/afghan-report.

Schneider, Gerald, Katherine Barbieri and Nils Petter Gleditsch (eds.) (2003) *Globalization and Armed Conflict* (Landham, MD: Rowman & Littlefield).

Schwartz, Peter, and Blair Gibb (1999) *When Good Companies Do Bad Things: Responsibility and Risk in the Age of Globalization* (New York: John Wiley).

Sedra, Mark (2002) *Challenging the Warlord Culture* (Bonn: Bonn International Center for Conversion).

Sen, Amartya (1997) 'Human Rights and Asian Values', Morgenthau Memorial Lecture, The New Republic, 14–21 July 1997.

—— (1999a) *Development as Freedom* (New York: Knopf).

—— (1999b) 'Democracy as a Universal Value', *Journal of Democracy* 10.3: 3-17.

Sim, H.C. Matthew (2001) *Myanmar on my Mind: A Guide to Living and Doing Business in Myanmar* (Singapore/Malaysia: Times Books International).

Transparency International (2004) *Global Corruption Report 2004*, www.globalcorruptionreport.org.

Trompenaars, Fons, and Charles Hampden-Turner (1998) *Riding the Waves of Culture* (New York: McGraw-Hill).

UN Global Compact (2001) *Business in Zones of Conflict: The Role of the Multinational in Promoting Regional Stability* (Juliette Bennett, International Peace Forum; www.unglobalcompact.org, March 2001).

—— (2002) *Business Guide on Conflict Impact Assessment*, www.unglobalcompact.org.

—— (2003) *The 21st Century NGO: In the Market for Change* (with SustainAbility and UNEP; www.unglobalcompact.org, June 2003).

—— (2004) *Assessing the Global Compact's Impact* (report by McKinsey, 9 June 2004).

UN Economic and Social Council, Commission on Human Rights (2003) *Draft Norms on the Responsibility of Transnational Companies and Other Business Enterprises with regard to Human Rights*, www1.umn.edu/humanrts/links/commentary-Aug2003.html.

UNEP FI (UN Environment Programme Finance Initiative) and IISD (International Institute for Sustainable Development) (2004) *Investing in Stability: Conflict Risk, Environmental Challenges and the Bottom-Line* (background paper, consultation version; www.unepfi.net/conflict/Investing%20in%20Stability_unepfi_iisd.pdf, June 2004).

WBCSD (World Business Council for Sustainable Development) (2002) *The Business Case for Sustainable Development*, www.wbcsd.org.

Webley, Simon, and Elise More (2003) *Does Business Ethics Pay?* (London: Institute of Business Ethics).

Wenger, Andreas, and Daniel Möckli (2003) *Conflict Prevention: The Untapped Potential of the Business Sector* (Boulder, CO: Lynne Rienner).

World Bank (2002) *Conflict, Peacebuilding and Development Cooperation: The World Bank Agenda*, www.worldbank.org.

—— *Public Sector Roles in Strengthening Corporate Social Responsibility: A Baseline Study*, www.worldbank.org.

—— (2003) *Company Codes of Conduct and International Standards: An Analytical Comparison*, www.worldbank.org.

—— (2003) *Jumpstarting Foreign Direct Investment: Generating a 'Peace Dividend' in Conflict-Affected Countries*, www.worldbank.org.

—— (2004) *Reforming Infrastructure: Privatization, Regulation and Competition*, www.worldbank.org.

Useful websites

News and discussion

- CSR Newswire Service: www.csrwire.com, mainly news from companies
- Corporate Social Responsibility, news and resources: www.mallenbaker.net, personal site of Mallen Baker, Development Director of Business in the Community
- Conversations with Disbelievers, www.conversations-with-disbelievers.net, website of AccountAbility and the Center for Corporate Citizenship of the Boston College with results of CSR
- Development Gateway, www.developmentgateway.org, news on development co-operation
- Reliefweb, www.reliefweb.int, news on relief operations
- Third World Network, www.twnside.org.sg

Corporate social responsibility

- AccountAbility, www.accountability.org.uk
- Business Action for Sustainable Development, Johannesburg 2002, basd.free.fr
- Business in the Community, www.bitc.org.uk
- Business for Social Responsibility, www.bsr.org

- Business and Sustainable Development, www.bsdglobal.com
- Corporate Social Responsibility Europe, www.csreurope.org
- Ethical Corporation, www.ethicalcorp.com
- Global Reporting Initiative, www.globalreporting.org
- Voluntary Principles on Security and Human Rights, www.state.gov/g/drl/rls/2931.htm
- World Bank, Private Sector Development, rru.worldbank.org/Themes/CorporateGovernance
- World Business Council for Sustainable Development, www.wbcsd.org

Non-governmental organisations

- Amnesty International, www.amnesty.org
- The Asia Foundation NGO–Business Environmental Partnership Program, www.asiafoundation.org
- Business and Human Rights Resource Centre, www.business-humanrights.org
- Campaign 'Publish What You Pay', www.publishwhatyoupay.org
- Civicus Corporate Engagement Program, www.civicus.org
- Civil Society International, www.civilsoc.org
- Global Witness, www.globalwitness.org
- Human Rights Watch, www.hrw.org
- International Alert, www.international-alert.org

Research

- Corporate Europe Observatory, www.corporateeurope.org, on the economic and political power of corporations
- Culture and Management Consulting, www.cmc-net.org, research on cultural differences in multinational corporations
- Focus on the Global South, www.focusweb.org, on the impact of globalisation
- Global Policy Forum, www.globalpolicy.org, 'watchdog' of the UN
- International Crisis Group, www.crisisgroup.org
- Logos Research, www.businessdiplomacy.biz, research on the contribution of multinational corporations in conflict prevention and resolution

Appendix
World map of conflict regions

The map overleaf shows regions of violent conflict (situation as per 1 May 2005). The map depicts only the 32 most severe conflicts (repeated and organised violence) and wars. In over 40 other conflicts violence occurs sporadically, or is asserted by only one party.

LATIN AMERICA
1. **Guatemala (FRG):** national power
2. **Haiti:** turmoil after political transition
3. **Colombia (ELN):** national power
   Colombia (FARC): national power
   Colombia (paramilitary): regional power

AFRICA
4. **Liberia:** national power
5. **Ivory Coast (rebels):** national power
6. **Togo:** national power
7. **Nigeria (Niger Delta):** resources
8. **Angola (Cabinda):** secession
9. **Democratic Republic of Congo (rebels):** national power, resources
   Democratic Republic of Congo (Hema contra Lendu): regional power, resources
10. **Burundi (Hutu):** national power
11. **Central African Republic (recurrent coups d'état):** national power
12. **Uganda (LRA):** national power
13. **Somalia:** national power
14. **Sudan (Darfur-SLA):** regional power

MIDDLE EAST
16. **Israel–Palestinian Territories:** autonomy
17. **Iraq:** regime change, regional power, resources
18. **Afghanistan (Taliban):** national power

ASIA
19. **Pakistan–India (Kashmir):** border conflict
20. **Nepal (rebels):** national power
21. **India (Kashmir):** secession
    India (Nagaland): secession
    India (Tripura): secession
    India–Pakistan (Kashmir): border conflict
22. **Sri Lanka (LTTE):** autonomy
23. **Myanmar/Burma (ethnic minorities):** autonomy
24. **Laos (rebels):** autonomy, national power
25. **Indonesia (Aceh):** secession, resources
26. **Philippines (rebels):** secession

Index

Abdullah, Abdullah 78
ABN Amro 15, 18
AccountAbility 132
Aceh 126
Action-oriented culture 32-34, 93-95
ADB
    see Asian Development Bank
Afghanistan 72-86, 95, 126
    contraband trade in 80
    corporate risks in 81-82
    Hawala system 72-73
    ING Group in 73-77, 81-86
    power structures in 77-79, 83-84
    UN economic sanctions 91
Afghanistan International Bank (AIB)
    73-77
Afghanistan Reconstruction Company
    (ARC) 81
Africa
    companies in conflict zones 16-17
    Heineken in 29, 38-53, 98-99
    violent conflicts in, 2005 136-37
    see also under individual countries
Aga Khan Foundation 74, 76
Agfa-Gevaert 62
Aguas de Barcelona 104
Alcatel 62
Algeria 16
American Enterprise Institute 105
Amnesty International 112, 114, 120
    Business Group 98, 103-104, 116
    website 133
Angkor Wat, Cambodia 118
Angola
    companies operating in, 16
    Total Energy in 54, 58, 59
    UN economic sanctions 90, 126
Annan, Kofi 19
Anti-globalisation movement 105
Apartheid 91, 96
Argentina 63

ASEAN (Association of South-East Asian
    Nations) 66, 71
Asia
    companies in conflict zones 17
    culture of 25, 28, 36-37, 64-67
    violent conflicts in 137
Asia Foundation 133
Asia Pacific Breweries 47
Asian Development Bank (ADB) 74, 77,
    81-82, 84
Aston, Ron 60-61
AT&T 17
Aung San, General 64, 67
Aung San Suu Kyi 56, 59, 60, 64-65, 67,
    69, 70
Australia 61, 121
Azerbaijan 17, 103-4

Baker, Mallen 132
Bangladesh 122
Bayer 21
Bekaert 21
Belgium 21, 62
Bhagwati, Jagdish 94
BHP Billiton 111
Bosnia 126
Boycotts
    see Sanctions
BP 16-17, 103-104, 120
Brazil 49
British Institute of Business Ethics 19
Brunei 66
Buddhism 63, 66-67, 117
Burma (Myanmar)
    and ASEAN 66, 71
    Buddhist/Confucian values of 65-67
    Corporate Engagement Project 107
    democracy in 56, 59, 60-61, 63-65, 71
    labour, forced 18, 54, 57, 58, 68
    opposition to trade with 35, 36, 47, 55-
        56, 59-60, 94

Premier Oil in   60-62, 98
and sanctions/isolation of   60-61, 62-
    63, 68-71, 96-97
Total Energy, operations in   54-62
tourism in   97, 117-25
    pitfalls of   122-24
    regulation/negotiation of   120-
        22, 125
Triumph in   59-60
warlords ceasefire agreements   95,
    123-24
Burundi, Africa
companies operating in,   17
Heineken in   38-41, 98-99
**Business Action for Sustainable
    Development**   132
**Business and Human Rights Resource
    Centre**   133
Business and Peace Conference   19
Business and Sustainable Development
    133
Business Ethics Forum   111
Business for Social Responsibility   120,
    132
Business Forum, Yangon   68-69
Business Humanitarian Forum (BHF)
    85
Business in the Community   132
Business Partners for Development
    102, 104, 112

Cambodia   66, 70
companies operating in,   17
tourism in   118
Cameroon   107
Canada   26, 94, 102
Care International   109
Carlsberg   62
Castro, Fidel   27-28, 87, 94, 96
Chad   17, 122
Chevron   120
Child labour   29, 49, 84
China   67, 69
and Burma, trade with   35, 36, 65, 120-
    21, 124
Civicus   133
Civil Society International   133
Civil wars
and economic performance   12-14
see also Conflict zones
Clinton, Bill   94
Coca-Cola   42, 80, 110
Codes of conduct   120
Collaborative Development Action   107

Colombia   88, 101-102
companies operating in,   16
Coltan mining   21-22
Columbia University   94
Commission for Human Rights   61
Compaq   62
'Conflict diamonds'   15, 18
'Conflict Risk and Impact Assessment'
    84
Conflict zones
companies in, 1990s   15-17
as at May 2005   136-37
Conflicts, inter-ethnic   45-47, 99
Confucianism   65
Congo, Democratic Republic of   38-39,
    44-45, 47, 51, 126
coltan mining in   21-22
companies operating in,   16
UN economic sanctions   91
Congo, Republic of   16
Congo-Kinshasa
see Congo, Democratic Republic of
Conoco   120
Consumer pressure   62
Conversations with Disbelievers   132
Corona-Lotus   21
Corporate Engagement Project   57, 107
Corporate Europe Observatory   134
Corporate social responsibility   31, 32
websites   132-33
Corporate Social Responsibility Europe
    133
CorporateWatch website   105
CorpWatch website   20, 105
Corruption   36, 122
Council on Economic Priorities (CEP)
    19
Croatia   16
Crystallex   102
CSR Newswire Service   132
Cuba
economic sanctions on   27-28, 87-88,
    94, 96, 126
tourism, impacts of   118
'Cultural intelligence'   23-25, 32
Culture   32-37
action-oriented   32-34, 93-95
Asian   25, 28, 36-37, 64-67
and ethics   24-25, 26-37
Latin   31-32
organisational   30, 106-7
process-oriented   32-34, 95-96
role-oriented   32, 33, 35-37
task-oriented   32, 33, 35-36

Culture and Management Consulting
134

Daimler-Benz AG   16
DaimlerChrysler   42
D'Amore, Louis   119
Daudzai, Umer   80
De Langavant, Olivier   54, 57, 58-59
Democracy
    and Asian culture   64-67
    in Burma (Myanmar)   56, 59, 60-61,
        63-65, 71
Development Gateway   132
DHL International   62
Diamonds   15, 18
Dian Fossey Gorilla Fund   22
Dostum, Abdul Rashid   78
Durban Process   22

Eastman-Kodak   62
Economic co-operation   54-71
    see also Sanctions
'Economic terrorism'   96-97
Ecopetrol   101
Education, and MNCs   43, 61-62
Egypt, tourism in   122
El Salvador   16
Elkington, John   110
Embargoes, trade/investment
    see Sanctions
'Equator Principles'   84
Eritrea   91
Esso   110
Ethical colonialism   25
Ethical Corporation   133
Ethics and culture   24-25, 26-37
    Asian   25, 28, 36-37
    international standards in   31-32
    in organisations   30, 106-7
    politics of   27-28
    power in   28-29
    see also Culture
Ethiopia   91
European Union
    and Cuba, policies on   28, 94
    political pressure by   60
    social development   102
Extractive industries
    codes of conduct   120
    and tripartite partnerships   103
ExxonMobil   16-17, 106

Fahim, Mohammad Qasim   78, 79
Fairfield University   93

Far Eastern Economic Review   96
Farchim   62
Fiorina, Carly   34
First Microfinance Bank   74
Forced labour   18, 54, 57, 58, 68, 99
Ford Corporation   16-17
FR Yugoslavia   91, 92
    see also Yugoslavia
Frankental, Peter   98, 103-104, 116
'Freedom,' concepts of   64-65, 77
Freeport-McRoRan   112, 120

Galtung, Johan   92
General Motors   16-17
Georgia   103-104
Ghani, Ashraf   76, 82-83
Gillette   80
GlaxoSmithKline   62
Global Compact   19-20, 110
Global Policy Forum   134
Global Reporting Initiative   133
Global Witness   133
Globalisation   105, 134
Gold mining   102, 107
Gorbachev, Michael   88
Gordon, Joy   93
Government
    and enterprise, roles of   38-53
    influencing   47-48
    and public tasks   22, 42-44
    see also Democracy; Military regimes
Greenpeace   106
Guatemala   16
Guidelines, international   120
Gulf Region   17

Hain, Peter   19
Haiti   90, 122, 126
Haley, Usha C.V.   91
Hawala system   72-73
H.C. Starck   21-22
Healthcare   43, 49, 102
    and HIV/AIDS   42, 43, 48
Heineken
    in Africa   29, 38-53, 98-99
    in Burma (Myanmar)   62
    and corporate social responsibility   31, 32
Hertz, Noreena   105
Hewlett-Packard   34
Hitachi   16
HIV/AIDS   42, 43, 48
Hobbs, Jeremy   111, 113-14
Homé, Jean-Louis   29, 31, 32, 38-48, 51-
    53, 98-99

Horsey, Richard 67
Hufbauer, Gary Clyde 89, 92
Human rights
    Burma (Myanmar) 59, 61
    Cuba 27-28
    Indonesia 112
    NGOs, websites 133
    Sudan 26-27
    voluntary principles on 120, 133
    see also Amnesty International
Human Rights Watch 120, 133
Hussein, Saddam 32, 92

IBM 16-17
IHC Caland 35
India 17, 88, 94
Indian Oil and Natural Gas Corporation 26-27
Indonesia 66, 88, 89, 111, 112
    companies operating in, 17
    government in 63
ING Group 73-77, 81-86
Institute for International Economics 89, 92
Interbrew 21, 62
Inter-ethnic conflicts 45-47, 99
International Alert 19, 21, 84, 133
International Chamber of Commerce 109
International Confederation of Free Trade Unions (ICFTU) 19
International Crisis Group 71, 134
International Finance Corporation 82, 84, 133
International Institute for Peace through Tourism 119
International Labour Organisation (ILO) 58-59, 67
International Monetary Fund (IMF) 45
International Security and Assistance Force (ISAF) 72, 74
International standards 31-32
Iran 67, 88, 94
Iraq
    companies operating in, 17
    economic sanctions on 89, 90, 92
    reconstruction of 24, 126
Israel 89, 92
Itochu 16-17
Ivory Coast 91, 126

Japan, and Burma 61, 66, 69, 121
Jordan, Bill 19-20

Kabbah, Ahmed Tejan 36
Kabul International Airport 72
Karzai, Hamid 73, 78, 79, 83
Kazakhstan 83
Kazemi, Mustafa 76, 78
Kinshasa, Africa 38
Kirk McDonald, Gabrielle 112
Klein, Naomi 105
Koramic Building Products 21
Kosovo 126
Kothari, Miloon 78-79
Kyrgyzstan 83

Labour
    child 29, 49, 84
    forced 18, 54, 57, 58, 68, 99
Laos 66
Latin America
    companies in conflict zones 16
    violent conflicts in, 2005 136-37
Lebanon 17
Liberia 126
    companies operating in, 16
    UN economic sanctions 90, 95
Libya 90, 94
'Licence to operate' 18-19, 84
Logos Research 134

Ma Thanegi 96-97
Magdalena Medio Regional Development Project 101-102
Mahbubani, Kishore 64
Malaysia 66
Mandela, Nelson 96
Maqsudi, Farid 80-81
Médecins sans Frontières 107
Microsoft 104
Middle East
    companies in conflict zones 17
    violent conflicts in, 2005 137
Military intervention 126
Military regimes, repressive
    isolating, strategy of 60-61, 62-63, 68-71
Mining industry 102, 103, 111, 112, 116
Mitsubishi 16-17
Mitsui 16-17
Mitterrand, Jean-Christophe 44
Mobil 16-17
Moldova 16
Money changers 72-73
Mongolia 75
Montaner, Carlos Alberto 87-88
Moody-Stuart, Mark 48-49

Morocco 89
Mozambique 21
Mugabe, Robert 95
Multinational corporations (MNCs) 12-25
    accountability of 115-16
    Asian, culture of 36-37, 60
    in conflict zones, 1990s 15-17
    'cultural intelligence' of 23-25, 32
    dilemmas of 22-23, 32
    'domain' boundaries of 48-50
    and economic sanctions 98-100
    and education, 43, 61-62
    and international standards 31-32
    and NGOs 101-16
        building confidence in 113-16
        comparison with 108
        distrust of 105-109
        partnerships, tripartite 50-53, 103-104
    organisational culture of 30, 106-7
    and public tasks 22, 38-53
    self-interest of 18-19
Myanmar
    see Burma
Myanmar Oil and Gas Enterprise (MOGE) 56, 58

Nadiri, Ishaq 81
National Bank of Pakistan 74
Nepal 107, 126
Nestlé 62, 80
New Light of Myanmar, The 63, 70
New York Times 64
New York University 81
NGOs
    see Non-governmental organisations
Nicaragua 21
Nigeria 95, 107, 122
    companies operating in, 16
    oil companies in 24
Nike 104
Nippon Telegraph and Telephone 17
Non-governmental organisations (NGOs)
    accountability of 115-16
    and diamond trade 15, 18
    and economic sanctions 94
    and MNCs 101-16
        comparison with 108
        confidence building 113-15
        distrust of 105-109
    organisational culture of 30, 106-107
    tripartite partnerships 50-53, 103-104

and water infrastructures 30
websites 133
see also Amnesty International; Oxfam

Oil industry
    in Burma 54-62
    and forced labour 18, 57-58
    and military, finance for 54, 58
    in Nigeria 24
    see also individual companies
Ondeo 49
Organisational cultures 30, 106-107
Ould Abdallah, Ahmedou 39-40, 48, 99
Oxfam International 110-11, 113-14

Pakistan 88, 89, 94
    companies operating in, 17
Palestinian Territories 126
Panama 126
Papua New Guinea 107, 116
Partnerships, tripartite 50-53, 103-104
    distrust in 105-9
    and organisational culture 106-107
Pe-Win, Bernard 68-69
'Peace agents', role of 125
Peace through Tourism, International Institute for 119
Perret-Nguyen, Hông-Trang 67-68
Personnel recruitment, influencing 29, 45-46
Peru 16
Petronas company 60, 61
Philippines 17, 66
Philips 62
Pierer, Heinrich von 20
Placer Dome 102
Premier Oil
    in Burma 60-62, 98
Prince of Wales Business Leaders Forum (PWBLF) 19
Process-oriented culture 32-34, 95-96
Procter & Gamble 80
'Profits versus ideals' 101-16
    and distrust 105-9
    and organisational culture 30, 106-107
    and partnerships, tripartite 50-53, 103-104
    reconciling dilemma 112-16
PTT EP 56
'Publish What You Pay' campaign 133

Qanuni, Yunos 78, 79

Racism 52-53
Rangoon (Yangon) 67-68
Reliefweb 132
Reputation, damage to 51-52, 57-58,
    100
Rio Tinto 120
Robert F. Kennedy Center on Human
    Rights 112
Role-oriented culture 32, 33, 35-37
Royal Dutch/Shell Group 16-17, 62, 110,
    120
  and child labour 49
  and NGOs 114-15
  in Nigeria 24
  and sustainable development 48-49
Roz Trading 80, 81
Russia 17, 137
Rwanda, Africa 38, 41
  companies operating in, 17
  UN economic sanctions 90

Sanctions, economic 27-28, 87-100,
    126
  and Burma, isolation of 60-61, 62-63,
    68-71, 96-97
  against Cuba 27-28, 87-88, 94, 96
  as 'economic terrorism' 96-97
  humanitarian side-effects of 92-93
  and multinational corporations 98-
    100
  and NGOs 94
  policies on
        in action-oriented cultures 93-95
        in process-oriented cultures 95-
        96
  'smart' 92-93
  UN Security Council 89-91
  US policies on 89, 92, 93-94, 95
Save the Children 61, 109
Schools, construction of 43, 48
Schott, Jeffrey 89, 92
Sein Thun 117
Sen, Amartya 25
Shell
    see Royal Dutch/Shell Group
Short, Clare 36
Sidmar 21
Siemens AG 16-17, 20, 21
Sierra Leone
  companies operating in, 16
  corruption in 36
  UN economic sanctions 91, 95
Simpson, Glenn 81
Singapore 64, 66

Somalia 91, 126
South Africa 89, 91, 96
  companies operating in, 17
Sri Lanka 17, 107
Stakeholders, communication with 52
Standard Chartered Bank 74
Statoil 21, 114
Strand Hotel, Yangon 68
Sudan 26-27, 115, 126
  companies operating in, 17
  UN economic sanctions 90
Sumitomo 16-17
SustainAbility 110

Tajikistan 17, 83
Talisman Energy Inc. 26-27
Tarnoff, Alexander 61
Task-oriented cultures 32, 33, 35-36
Tax collection 45
Taylor, Charles 95
Texaco 120
Thailand 66
  and Burma 124
  tourism in 118, 124
Third World Network 132
Torture, defining 25
Total Energy
  in Burma 54-62
Tourism 97, 117-25
  impacts of 117-19
  pitfalls of 122-24
  regulation of 120-21
Tourism, International Institute for
    Peace through 119
Tourism Concern 119
Toyota 16-17
Transparency
  lack of, in Asian MNCs 60
  in personnel recruitment 29, 45-46
  and trust, gaining 52, 84-85
Transparency International 122
Triumph 59-60
Trust, gaining 52, 61, 84-85
  between MNCs/NGOs 113-15
Turkey 89, 103-4
  companies operating in 17
Turkmenistan 83

U Win Aung 63, 70
Uganda 17
Ul-Haq Ahady, Anwar 76, 79
Unilever 42, 111
Union Minière 21
United Kingdom 60, 89, 93

United Nations
  Development Programme   80, 85
  Environment Programme   110
  Global Compact   19-20, 110
  Human Rights Commission   26
  Security Council   20
    economic sanctions by   89-93
United States
  and Cuba, policies on   27-28, 87-88,
    94, 96, 118
  and economic sanctions   89, 92, 93-94,
    95
UNOCAL   56, 65
Usine Chimique Belge (UCB)   62
Utilities, regulation of   50
  see also Water supplies
Uzbekistan   80, 81, 83

Van Dijken, Arno   74-77, 79, 81-82
Van Dooremalen, Sjef   35
Venezuela   21, 102
Vietnam   66
Violent conflict zones
  companies in, 1990s   15-17
  as at May 2005   136-37
Vivendi Water   49
Voluntary Principles on Security and
  Human Rights   120, 133

WAC Global Services   24
Wal-Mart   17
Wars
  see Civil wars; Conflict zones
Water supplies   30, 49, 102
Websites, useful   132-34
Westgaard, Geir   114
Wijbrandi, Jan Bouke   111
World Bank   45, 80
  and Colombia   101-102
  and utilities, regulation of   49-50
World Business Council for Sustainable
  Development (WBCSD)   20-21, 133
World Trade Organisation   109
Wrigley   80

Yadana gas project   56-57
Yakubie, Zaher   81
Yangon (Rangoon)   67-68
Yemen   17
Yetagun gas project   60
Yugoslavia   16, 90
  see also FR Yugoslavia

Zandvliet, Luc   107-109, 113-16
Zimbabwe   88, 95

For Product Safety Concerns and Information please contact our
EU representative GPSR@taylorandfrancis.com Taylor & Francis
Verlag GmbH, Kaufingerstraße 24, 80331 München, Germany